Y0-DWL-905

The Spy Who Fell to Earth

The Spy Who Fell to Earth

MY RELATIONSHIP WITH
THE SECRET AGENT WHO
ROCKED THE MIDDLE EAST

———

Ahron Bregman

Copyright © 2016 Ahron Bregman
All rights reserved.

ISBN: 1523229977
ISBN 13: 9781523229970
Library of Congress Control Number: 2016900454
CreateSpace Independent Publishing Platform
North Charleston, South Carolina

About the Author

———

Photo by Murdo MacLeod

AHRON (RONNIE) BREGMAN WAS BORN in 1958 in Israel, where he served in the army, reached the rank of captain and took part in the 1982 war in Lebanon. In the late 1980s, he left Israel in protest at the military's violent suppression of the Palestinian uprising (the *intifada*) against the Israeli occupation and settled in the UK, where he completed a doctorate in War Studies. He is the author of *The Fifty Years War* (with Jihan el-Tahri), the companion book to a six-part BBC / PBS television documentary, *Elusive Peace*, the companion book to a three-part BBC / PBS television documentary, *Israel's Wars, A History of Israel* and *Cursed Victory*. Ahron teaches at King's College London. He lives in Kingston-upon-Thames.

For
Ashraf Marwan,
who deserved a better end

Contents

'*What do you think spies are: priests, saints, martyrs?*
They're a squalid procession of vain fools, traitors, too …
people who play cowboys and Indians to brighten their
rotten lives.'

John le Carré, The Spy Who Came in
from the Cold

'*I am not a superman.*'

Ashraf Marwan to Ahron Bregman

The End

——

THERE ARE MOMENTS IN A man's life which are imprinted on his mind and which he carries with him to the end. For me one such a moment is remembered in particular; that was when I learned of the brutal death of Ashraf Marwan, an Egyptian who worked as a Mossad spy.

His name was top secret until I unmasked him in December 2002. But what at first seemed to be a moment of glory and the pinnacle of my professional career – being the first historian to reveal and write in detail on Israel's most senior spy ever, and perhaps the most important spy in the history of modern espionage – turned out to be a sheer nightmare, as a few years later he died in mysterious circumstances. Even now, years after the event, I can still – almost physically – relive the moment I was told of his death. My mobile phone rings. An overseas telephone call, and then a short exchange:

'Have you heard what has happened?'

'Heard what?'

'He's dead.'

'Who's dead?'

'Marwan … Ashraf Marwan … he fell off a balcony … he was either pushed or jumped.'

I am standing in the middle of a field, my usual short cut on my way back home from work, my head spinning, and I am stunned to the core, struggling to collect myself. That day I was due to meet up with Marwan in town. He phoned the day before. Something was wrong; he sounded anxious and shaken. We arranged to meet up near King's College London, where I teach. But when he failed to phone again as we'd arranged the day before – to see where and when exactly we would meet – I gave up waiting for him and returned home. And now the dreadful news!

For a long time now friends would enquire why I did not write the story of my relationship with Ashraf Marwan; after all, it was stranger than a tale of fiction, for soon after I had unmasked him as a top Mossad spy, Marwan made contact and we then kept in touch for almost five years. We met face to face, spoke frequently on the phone; he even made me his consultant on memoirs he was writing, which, as I would learn, mysteriously vanished on the day he plunged to his death.

Why, of all people, Marwan chose to become friends with me – the man who had exposed him as a spy in the first place – is still a mystery even to me, though I do have some thoughts about it which I will discuss later. As the Marwan affair turned out to be so traumatic for me I was, for years, reluctant to touch it. But now – at fifty-seven – I realize just how close I am to Marwan's age when he plunged to earth and died, and I am starting to acknowledge my own mortality.

Putting the story of my relationship with Marwan on paper has not been difficult. From the day he picked up the phone and spoke to me for the first time, I realized that instead of being merely a historian whose task it is to record events, I somehow had become an active participant in them; though, as I would soon learn, it is easier to write history than to make it, even in such a mild way as mine. I therefore kept recording my dealings with Marwan by summarizing our significant telephone conversations, keeping faxes I had sent to him and recordings of two significant – indeed extraordinary – telephone calls: one a tape with three messages Marwan had left on my answering machine the day before he died, and a subsequent telephone conversation I made with him and which I secretly recorded. This material is now deposited at the Liddell Hart Archives at King's College London, and much of it has been used to write this book.

Part I

CHAPTER 1

Who was Ashraf Marwan?

——

ASHRAF MARWAN WAS AN EGYPTIAN who moved in his country's ruling political and power circles. He married the daughter of the great Arab leader Gamal Abdel Nasser, the ruler of Egypt from 1954 until his death in 1970. Nasser was succeeded by his deputy, Anwar al-Sadat, who turned Marwan into his right-hand man, and in this role Marwan accompanied Sadat on the most sensitive missions and was present in critical meetings in and outside Egypt, particularly in the period leading up to the 1973 Yom Kippur War between Israel and Egypt. Being so close to the two presidents made Marwan privy to Egypt's most sensitive secrets. But Marwan was living a double life – for at the same time he was serving Nasser and Sadat, he also worked for Egypt's sworn enemy, Israel, as a top spy for the Mossad, Israel's intelligence agency.

He was born Mohammad Ashraf Abu el Wafa Marwan in 1944 in Cairo into a respected middle-class family, one of four children of an army officer. Ashraf was a bright and ambitious pupil who excelled in science and was an avid reader, always carrying books he had borrowed from the local library and often found sitting in corners immersing himself in stories from across the world. Upon finishing high school with top grades he went straight to university to study chemistry, instead of joining the military as most youngsters did in Egypt. In 1965, with a university degree under his belt, Marwan joined the Egyptian army as an officer and chemical engineer. It is then that his life changed for ever: he met and fell in love with Mona, three years his junior, and the third, most beautiful, daughter of President Nasser.

Mona was a student at the Faculty of Economics and Political Science at the American University in Cairo and the first encounter between her and Ashraf Marwan took place on the beach in Alexandria. It was not an accidental meeting, but was arranged by Marwan's young sister Uzz, who was Mona Nasser's good friend.[1] Love flowered but when President Nasser heard about his daughter's new match he was not impressed, and his doubts were confirmed when his head of bureau, a certain Sami Ashraf, produced a less-than-flattering intelligence report on Marwan, portraying him as a playboy and a reckless opportunist. However, Nasser's efforts to dissuade his daughter from seeing Marwan were in vain, as she had fallen deeply in love with this charming, dashing, good-looking man. Reluctantly, Nasser gave his permission for them to wed.

On 7 July 1966 the two married in what turned out to be the most glittering social event of the year in Cairo. The entire Egyptian elite attended and the great Egyptian singer Umm Kol Tum, renowned across the Middle East for her beautiful voice, entertained the guests. A picture released to the press after the wedding shows a smiling Marwan shaking hands with his father-in-law, Nasser, on his right Mona in a beautiful white wedding dress, looking at her father, almost pleading for his approval.

Ashraf Marwan (Right) on his wedding day with his bride Mona Abdel Nasser, daughter of late Egyptian president Gamal Abdel Nasser (Left), Cairo, 7 July 1966. © PA Images

After the wedding the young couple remained in Cairo. Nasser still mistrusted his new son-in-law and, to keep an eye on him, he appointed Marwan to a job at the Presidential Information Bureau, which at the time was the regime's nerve centre. Here he'd be supervised by Sami Ashraf – the man who'd written the unflattering intelligence report on Marwan.

Soon Mona gave birth to a son, and while Nasser adored his mischievous grandson, Gamal, it still failed to improve his relationship with his son-in-law. Even worse, life close to the suspicious, overwhelming president, whom Marwan would call 'Father Gamal', and having to spend long hours working under the prying eye of Sami Ashraf, who Marwan knew kept reporting back to Nasser, placed great strain on Marwan's relationship with Mona. On top of that, the couple also had money worries: while Mona had to stop working to look after baby Gamal, Marwan's salary of less than 100 Egyptian lira a month, while reasonable, only allowed for a fairly basic standard of living.

Marwan and Mona might have lived their lives out quietly in Cairo had not one of the Arab world's most cataclysmic events happened the year after their marriage. In 1967, Egypt and her Arab allies suffered an overwhelming defeat in the June Six Day War with Israel. The war was a disaster for Egypt – and for Nasser in particular. It had been the Egyptian president whose diplomatic brinkmanship had caused the war, a war in which Egypt lost the entire Sinai desert and Nasser's Arab allies – Jordan and Syria – also lost vast tracts of land, including the holy sites important for the Muslim world in Arab East

Jerusalem. Nasser took personal responsibility for the catastrophe and offered his resignation while the war was still going on, but this was rejected by the Egyptian people who still regarded him as their ultimate leader. His wife, Tahia, describes in her memoirs, *Nasser: My Husband*, how, after giving his speech of resignation, Nasser came back home 'took off his suit and put on his pajamas, and lay down on the bed', but then 'the road was blocked with people and ... many of them were crying openly, some sitting on the stairs weeping ... the sound of the crowds was beyond imagination'. Later, Mona came to her mother and said that she had heard that 'father has agreed to remain as President'.[2] So Nasser stayed as the president, but he never really recovered from the 1967 disaster he had brought on Egypt and the Arab world, and for those living close to him – such as Marwan and Mona – life became unbearable.

To escape, Marwan and Mona decided to get out of Cairo and settle for a while in the UK, with the excuse that there Ashraf could begin studying for a Master's degree in chemistry. Nasser was reluctant – Mona was his favourite daughter and he wanted her close to him; he also still did not trust his son-in-law. But if there was one thing the great Gamal Abdel Nasser could not possibly resist, it was the pleas of Mona, who would often get her mother on her side to pressurize Nasser; so when Mona kept nagging him – in fact begging him – to let her and Ashraf travel to England, Nasser reluctantly agreed.

———

For the young couple, relocation to London was a cultural shock. London was the world capital of cool, a city associated with all things hip and fashionable that had been growing in the popular imagination throughout the decade. It was one of the world's most dynamic cities, a fashion and cultural scene that was such a contrast to the gloomy Cairo they had left behind.

They settled in a tiny apartment and lived on a small allowance organized for them by Nasser, which Marwan topped up with money he earned at the Egyptian embassy in a position imposed on him by the president as a way to keep an eye on him. Nasser, as it soon emerged, had good reason to suspect that his young son-in-law might find it difficult to resist London's offers and temptations. Indeed, as money was short, Marwan looked for an easy way to get it. He charmed a lady by the name of Soad, a poet who was also the young wife of Abdullah al Mubarak al-Sabbah, a rich Kuwaiti oil sheik, and she provided Marwan with cash. Later, she would explain that it was wrong for the daughter of the admired President Nasser, her husband and Nasser's little grandchild to live a life of poverty in London. True, perhaps, but the money, rather than being used to support his family, was spent by Marwan at the gaming tables in London's casinos.[3] Unfortunately for Marwan, the story soon reached his furious father-in-law, who ordered Marwan's return to Cairo 'on the next flight'. So Marwan was put in the Egyptian ambassador's car, driven to the airport, and accompanied to the steps of the aeroplane to Cairo, where, as the plane landed, a car was waiting to take him straight to a meeting with Nasser. Reports of the incident describe Marwan's face to have been as 'white as a sheet' and that he was 'trembling like a leaf' when standing before his furious father-in-law. Nasser summarily demanded that Marwan divorce his daughter, which Mona refused to accept. When things calmed down a bit new arrangements were put in place: Marwan would pay back the money he had received from the Kuwaiti sheik's wife and the couple would return to live in Egypt; Marwan would go back to work at the Presidential Information Bureau in Cairo, where Sami Ashraf could keep an eye on him. As for London, Marwan would fly back there only to hand in his course papers and sit his exams.

CHAPTER 2

Marwan Volunteers
for the Mossad

―――

THE CAIRO THE MARWANS ENCOUNTERED on their forced return was even more depressing than the place they had left
a couple of years before. Egypt had not yet recovered from
the consequences of the 1967 military defeat and meanwhile
a new, low-level war was also raging. The so-called 'War of
Attrition' took place around the Suez Canal, where Egyptian
and Israeli troops fired at each other and launched raids on
either side of the waterway. Hundreds were killed and injured,
particularly on the Egyptian side. Thousands abandoned the
towns and cities along the Suez Canal which were hit by Israeli
shells and marched on Cairo. This all soured the atmosphere
in the capital, and for the Marwans the abrupt shift from lively
London to gloomy Cairo was unbearable. We can never know
for sure whether it was this suffocating atmosphere, or his
personal despair and hopeless relationship with his imposing

father-in-law, that eventually drove the 26-year-old Ashraf Marwan to take a step that would alter the course of his life for ever, and have a profound impact on Middle Eastern history.

In July 1970, when back in London on one of his study visits, Marwan walked into a red telephone box, dialled the number of the Israeli embassy and asked to speak with someone from Israeli Intelligence. He was transferred to the military attaché's office, identified himself and explained that he wanted to work for Israeli Intelligence. The Israeli on the other end of the line failed to recognize that the person he was talking to was President Nasser's son-in-law, and as Marwan refused to leave his number there was no follow-up.

Anwar Sadat, President of Egypt from 1970 to 1981, turned Ashraf Marwan into his right-hand man

In Egypt, a couple of months later, President Nasser died of a massive heart attack. Although only fifty-two, Nasser had been sick for some time and the pressure of office took its toll on him. He was succeeded by his deputy, Anwar al-Sadat, a relatively unknown figure who was ridiculed in Egypt (and throughout the Middle East) and dubbed 'the dark donkey' on account of his Sudanese ancestry. When Nasser was president, Ashraf Marwan had been little more than a low-level clerk, but under Nasser's successor he would rise to the top, becoming Sadat's special emissary on the most sensitive diplomatic missions, particularly to Saudi Arabia and Libya.

Marwan's rise was all to do with Egyptian politics. Sadat had not expected to become president, and so his embrace of Marwan was a calculated move as he recognized the need to have someone from the Nasser clan on his side, to give the impression that his succession was approved by the former regime. Of course, the public was not aware of the complex relationship between Marwan and Nasser, as the tension between the two had always been kept private. As for Marwan, with his sharp instincts he identified an opportunity to build himself up, and he did all he could to serve his new master well. So, soon after Nasser's death, Marwan gained access to his father-in-law's private safe, from which he removed key intelligence documents containing sensitive information on powerful people in Egyptian society, which he handed over to Sadat.[1] For Sadat, this was a godsend – it enabled the new president to manoeuvre against his enemies, to lock some of them up, distance himself from others, and to survive the early difficult years of his presidency.

When, in December 1970, Marwan returned to London on another of his study trips, he was in a much stronger position than he had ever been under his late father-in-law, and confident that he could offer Israeli Intelligence something they would find difficult to resist. So he tried his luck again, once more phoning the Israeli embassy from a telephone box and offering to work for them. This time, unlike his previous attempt, Marwan left a contact telephone number, though he rejected an invitation to go to the Israeli embassy in person to discuss the matter, saying that such a visit could put his life in danger.

This time, the penny finally dropped and the Israelis realized who the mysterious caller actually was. It happened purely by chance. Two top spymasters were visiting London, Rehaviah Vardi, head of Tzomet, the Mossad department in charge of intelligence gathering from human sources, and Shmuel Goren, based in Brussels and in charge of all Mossad operations in Western Europe. Their London visit was almost over and they were already in the car on their way to Heathrow airport, when the Israeli military attaché with them in the car mentioned, in passing, a certain 'Arab guy' who kept phoning to offer his services. When the attaché spelled out the name of the mysterious 'Arab guy' – Ashraf Marwan – the two spymasters were stunned, as they knew, at once, that he was none other than the son-in-law of Egypt's former president, and Sadat's right-hand man. Incidentally, Marwan had been in the Mossad's sights for some time, particularly since his arrival in London to study, as a potential recruit thanks to his links to the Nasser family; but those at the Mossad responsible for recruitment thought it would be too difficult to procure someone as senior as Marwan to work for Israel. But now – a stroke of luck – here he was offering his services of his own volition![2]

So they cancelled their flights, turned back and without even reporting to their Tel Aviv headquarters, as was the practice in such cases, decided to make contact with Marwan. They were seasoned enough to know that if things sounded too good to be true they usually were, but they also knew that such opportunities must be grabbed, otherwise they often disappear for good. Both were experienced Intelligence agents – they were fully aware that Marwan might try to mislead them. After all, he was what in the espionage world one would call a 'walk-in', namely a person who volunteers rather than being recruited to work for a spying agency. Walk-ins are notorious for being double agents, deceivers whose real loyalty remains with those who send them in the first place.[3] But the temptation to recruit a person who was so close to the Egyptian president and to the heart of the Egyptian regime was just too great, and the two Mossad operators decided to take their chance. Subsequently, Marwan, still in London, received a phone call informing him that a meeting would soon be arranged and that he should await instructions and not stray from his telephone; a number was also given to him for use in an emergency.

Time was too short for the two Mossad operators to bring to London one of their experienced case officers to meet Marwan, so the choice fell on a certain Dubi Asherov, the second man in the Mossad station in London under the station commander, Rafi Meidan, operating from inside the Israeli embassy. He was in his mid-thirties, tall, slim, blue-eyed, Israeli-born but with good European manners who joined the Mossad just before the 1967 war. His English was perfect, with no hint at all of the usually heavy Israeli accent, and he was also fluent in Arabic, which was important as, at this stage, it was not yet clear whether Marwan could speak good enough English and what language he would prefer to use in his meeting with the Israelis.

As the day of the first meeting between Marwan and the Mossad loomed the Israelis were anxious. They feared a trap. Unbeknownst to the British authorities, armed Mossad agents surrounded the hotel where the rendezvous was due to take place, ready to break in to rescue their spies if needed. The opening scene of the film based on John le Carré's *Tinker, Tailor, Soldier, Spy* demonstrates, in a most dramatic fashion, how a British agent falls victim to such a trap set up by Russian spies, and the deadly consequences of his mistake.

In the hotel lobby, just before the meeting, Shmuel Goren, wearing a dark suit, positioned himself on a sofa facing the entrance, holding a copy of *The Times* inside which he pressed a four-year-old, quite blurry picture, taken from an Arabic newspaper, of Marwan during his wedding to Mona Nasser. As the minutes passed and Marwan did not appear, the Israelis inside and outside the hotel became nervous and alert. Finally, a tall, slim, smooth-faced, well-dressed gentleman walked in, holding a black document bag. Goren glanced down at the picture and compared it to the rakish man who had just walked through the front door; after a split-second's hesitation, he signalled to Dubi Asherov, standing nearby, that this was his man. Asherov approached Marwan, stretched out his hand and said in Arabic, 'Mr Marwan. It's good to meet you. I am Alex', Alex being an alias. Marwan was taken aback as he did not expect to hear Arabic and he replied in English, whereby Asherov at once switched to English, inviting Marwan to join him in a private room. The man with the newspaper, Shmuel Goren, folded the paper, collected his winter coat and left the building unnoticed.

Away from prying eyes and more relaxed, Marwan did his utmost to impress upon Asherov what he had to offer. He pulled out a sheaf of papers and started reading, translating it into English. Asherov was impressed, as what Marwan now described in minute detail was the Egyptian Order of Battle: the commands, formations and units of the Egyptian army, as well as the weapons used by the various units. Asherov, busy taking notes, stopped Marwan from time to time to ask for clarifications. Marwan also handed over to Asherov a sealed brown envelope that contained documents.

Marwan did not ask for anything in return, as for now all he wished to do was to impress. He said that in a few weeks' time he would return to London on yet another study trip and he'd then make contact with Asherov again. He made it clear that in the next meeting, and in those which might follow, the only person he would have contact with would be Asherov. The two men had hit it off; Asherov was a bit older than Marwan, but not much, and Marwan felt quite comfortable with the Israeli. He also wanted as few people as possible involved in the meetings, as the fewer people knew about him, the more secure he would be. When the meeting was over, they shook hands and Marwan left first, hailing a black cab, which was then followed by Mossad agents eager to see with whom he would meet next. They knew they had a potential treasure – a direct link to the heart of the Egyptian leadership – but they were also suspicious. A few minutes later Dubi Asherov emerged from the hotel and took a cab to the Israeli embassy, where he met Goren. Together they opened Marwan's envelope and closely inspected its top secret documents. Looking up at Asherov, Goren said, 'Material like this from a source like this is something that happens once in a thousand years.'

In Tel Aviv the next day, the Mossad's chiefs called a meeting to discuss Marwan. It was presided over by the Mossad's chief, Zvi Zamir. He was a 45-year-old former general who had participated in all Israel's wars since 1948 and was brought to the Mossad as an outsider to lead them thanks to his excellent organizational talents and dedication. Also present were Goren and Vardi, the two agents who had organized the London meeting with Marwan. The key question facing them was whether Marwan was genuinely interested in working for Israel, or whether he was a Trojan horse, dispatched by Egyptian Intelligence to penetrate the ranks of the Mossad. Was he planning to become a double agent in order to feed Israel incorrect information, or to pass secrets back to Sadat?

For hours the discussion went back and forth. Finally, they concluded that Marwan was genuine. Three things persuaded them to take a chance on him. First, the handling of double agents requires considerable subtlety, as the double agent is a tricky customer and needs careful supervision. Only

Mossad's chief, Zvi Zamir, who ordered Marwan's recruitment to the Mossad and often met with Marwan in London

very professional intelligence agencies – like the KGB and the British – were good at handling double agents for a long period of time; the Israelis thought that the Mukhabarat, the Egyptian intelligence agency, was not sophisticated enough to carry out such a task. Secondly, from an Egyptian point of view, using the former president's son-in-law and his successor's right-hand man as a spy carried immense risks; he could be killed or taken prisoner by the Israelis. Thirdly, in his first meeting with the Israelis in London, Marwan had handed over high-level information that the Israelis believed Egyptian intelligence would not have handed over, not even in order to persuade the Mossad to accept Marwan as their spy.[4] But if

Marwan was genuine, the Israelis were still unsure of his motive. Why? Why spy for them? Money, they were convinced, could be a reason. A thirst for adventure could be another. Marwan himself provided another motive, one that he gave Dubi Asherov at their London meeting: the Arabs had been humiliated by their defeat in 1967, Marwan said, and now he wanted to be on the side of the victors.

The Israelis concluded that Marwan was playing straight, and Zamir wrapped up the Tel Aviv meeting and authorized the organization to officially recruit Marwan to the Mossad. Normally, Mossad spies in Europe were handled by Shmuel Goren's office in Brussels. But Marwan was big enough for Tel Aviv to want to take him over themselves and for Zamir to be directly involved in his handling. As for the young Dubi Asherov, he would continue as Marwan's London case officer, responsible for the day-to-day running of Marwan; although Zamir had wished to put a more experienced case officer in charge of Marwan, it was apparent that Asherov and Ashraf had good chemistry and, moreover, it would be too risky to try and change Asherov – Marwan had made it absolutely clear that he would work only with the man he knew as 'Alex'. Finally, Zamir and his aides gave Marwan a cover name – 'The Angel', after the popular British TV series *The Saint*, which in Hebrew is translated as 'The Angel'; a nickname showing the near-celestial regard with which the Israelis viewed their new recruit.[5]

CHAPTER 3

Spying

———

THE MOSSAD, THOUGH, WERE STILL cautious. The Israelis had to be sure Marwan was not playing a double game, that he was not a deceiver. And they had one surefire way to do so – to weigh what he gave them against what they received from another agent deep within the Egyptian establishment. This agent – whose identity is still an Israeli state secret – was an Egyptian army officer who was controlled not by the Mossad but by Israeli Army Intelligence and provided superb information, particularly on the southern sector of the Egyptian front but also on other more general matters. And when the Mossad weighed, with painful care, the information they received from their two Egyptian spies, they concluded that Marwan was the real deal and that they had hit a gold mine, as was vividly demonstrated in 1971.

In August of that year Marwan handed over to his Mossad control, Dubi Asherov, one of Egypt's most closely held secrets – her top secret war plans. It outlined how five Egyptian infantry divisions, supported by armoured brigades, would cross the Suez Canal using small boats and bridges, establish a foothold on the east bank of the Canal and from there move deeper into the Sinai desert to liberate it from Israeli occupation. Marwan's information also included detailed maps, even transcripts of high-level Egyptian–Soviet meetings – the Soviets being the patrons of Egypt at that time, providing them with weapons and training. Marwan did something else too: he explained and interpreted the documents to the Israelis. The latter oral explanations were filed by the Mossad under the heading 'The Evaluation of the Source', the 'Source' being Ashraf Marwan, whose name was not spelled out in order to protect him. Marwan's evaluations focused on a range of military and political matters, and also on such general subjects as the Egyptian economy, education, top appointments to key posts in the Egyptian administration and gossip too. Trusted by his direct boss, President Sadat, Marwan was often dispatched as the president's representative to key meetings, notably of the Egyptian military high command, and straight after these meetings he provided the Israelis with transcripts of what happened, and he also described the atmosphere in these gatherings. For Israel, with Marwan's information under her belt, Egypt had become an open book, and, as a Mossad operator who often read Marwan's reports once put it, 'having Marwan as a spy was like being in bed with President Sadat'.[1]

As Marwan's information came from the very heart of the Egyptian leadership, Zvi Zamir, director of the Mossad, took an unusual step: he distributed Marwan's original reports –

translated into Hebrew – directly to a small circle of top decision-makers in Israel, primarily the prime minister, Golda Meir, the defence minister, Moshe Dayan, and the Army Chief of Staff, David Elazar; to protect Marwan's identity his information came under the codename 'Kotel', though everyone there knew who 'Kotel' actually was. In normal circumstances information gathered by the Mossad, even from their top sources, would pass through 'filters': it would first go to Military Intelligence and they would produce reports *based* on the raw material, which would then be distributed to key decision-makers. But with Marwan, Zamir felt that the procedure should be different, as giving his material in its raw form to the top political level, unencumbered by analysis, could help the prime minister, her ministers and key advisers to better understand how the Egyptian mind really worked.

———

As Marwan's reputation grew, the Israelis, who regarded him as such a miraculous source, recast their entire thinking about the probability of war with Egypt exclusively on the basis of Marwan's documents and his oral explanations and interpretations. This new thinking became known as 'The Conception'.

Rivers of ink have been spilled over the Israeli Conception, but in fact it is quite simple: at its heart was the understanding, based on Marwan's information, that Egypt would not wage war against Israel without first acquiring from her patrons, the Soviets, certain weaponry, namely fighter bombers with a capacity sufficient to drop large bombs on Israeli cities, and Scud missiles to deter the superior Israeli air force from attacking Egyptian centres of population, lest Israel retaliate in kind. Additionally, Egypt would not launch war against Israel on her own without direct Syrian participation too, as only simultaneous attacks, from south and north, could defeat Israel, by obliging the Israeli Defence Forces to be split (and thus weakened) in order to face assaults on two fronts.

Adhering to the Conception meant that, practically, all Israel had to do was monitor Egyptian airbases and other entry points into the country for evidence that these weapons, the aircraft and the missiles – Sadat's precondition to attack Israel, according to Marwan – had arrived in Egypt. So long as Egypt had not received the Soviet arms and aircraft it was desperate for, Israel could feel that it was safe from war. That this thinking (which later came under intense criticism, as Sadat would wage war anyway, without waiting for the weapons to arrive) was not a mere theory invented by the Israelis themselves, but came entirely from their top spy, Ashraf Marwan, we know from none other than Moshe Dayan, Israel's legendary defence minister in the early 1970s. The Conception was not, he said, an idea invented by 'a mad-genius in Israel's military establishment', but 'emerged from very critical information which we thought was the *best* one could have acquired' – a reference to information acquired from Marwan, though Dayan stopped short of spelling out Marwan's name as this was still one of Israel's most guarded secrets. Dayan added: 'I can say in full confidence that any intelligence agency in the world …

who would have known how the information was obtained would have trusted it' – again, an indirect reference to Ashraf Marwan being the source of the information.[2]

———

Most of the meetings with his control, Dubi Asherov, were initiated by Marwan. The Israelis, though, assumed that the telephone lines of their London embassy were tapped, by either British or other intelligence agencies, so they set up a system whereby Marwan would not have to endanger himself by phoning the embassy directly. Instead, he was given the telephone numbers of two London Jewish ladies who were working for the Mossad, and whenever he wished to meet 'Alex' he would phone one of them and leave an agreed code which they then forwarded to Asherov.[3] When the spy and his handler met up it was in a plush safe apartment near the Dorchester Hotel, which the Mossad purchased in 1971 solely for the purpose of talking to Marwan. Dubi Asherov often arrived at these meetings holding a suitcase containing thousands of banknotes, payment for Marwan's services; altogether Marwan would receive more than $1m from the Mossad – a staggeringly large amount for an intelligence source. And as Marwan and Asherov came to know each other better – they often met twice a month – the relationship between them became closer, even intimate, and from time to time they gave each other presents. As Marwan loved guns, particularly small pistols, he often brought them to the meetings, pointing them here and there; on one occasion, he gave Asherov a .38 Smith & Wesson pistol as a present. Asherov tried to dissuade Marwan from carrying guns, as even the British police did not carry weapons on the streets of London, but Marwan just laughed it off, saying to Asherov that 'nobody, but nobody, touches Ashraf Marwan'.[4]

This and other similar incidents reinforced the view in Tel Aviv that they had a problem: their top spy, Marwan, was reckless, and the problem was not only his obsession with guns but what seemed to be most irresponsible behaviour. Often, he would arrive at meetings with the Mossad driven in a car belonging to the Egyptian embassy and carrying a diplomatic number plate. On other occasions he phoned the Israeli embassy directly rather than resorting to the arrangement of using the go-between service of the Jewish ladies. And some of the documents he brought to the meetings were not even copies, but originals, stamped with a security classification and numbered, which, of course, could risk his neck should anyone in Egypt find out that the documents were missing.

The closer the relations between Marwan and Asherov become, the more concerned Zvi Zamir grew that this might hinder Asherov's ability to control Marwan efficiently. So Zamir ruled that Asherov should introduce Marwan to a successor. The choice fell on a Syrian-born Mossad agent, a charming, well-built man and an experienced operator.[5] But Marwan bridled and the idea was shelved, though not for long. A few months later, Zamir again instructed Asherov to introduce someone else, but this time round not to tell Marwan in advance; Asherov was to bring the replacement to the meeting and introduce him to Marwan there and then. The chosen man was an Iraqi-born Mossad operator, who waited in an adjacent room for a signal from Asherov to join the meeting. When he finally walked into the room, Marwan was taken aback and ignored the new man, who nonetheless tried to impress Marwan by talking to him in fluent Arabic, though with a hint of an Iraqi accent. When later the man left the room, Marwan turned to Asherov, complained about 'this Iraqi guy' and then, with an air of superiority, explained to Asherov that in the Arab world there is a hierarchy: at the top are the Egyptians, under them the Syrians, then the Jordanians and the Saudis; as for the Iraqis, 'they are at the bottom of the heap'. To emphasize his point, Marwan made a gesture of stepping on an insect.[6] With the second failed attempt to replace Dubi Asherov, the idea to find him a replacement was dropped for good, and to the end of his service with the Mossad Asherov – 'Alex' – would remain Ashraf Marwan's controller.

———

By now, Marwan had become so important to Israel that every care was taken to keep him happy. When Dubi Asherov learned that relations between Marwan and his wife, Mona, were shaky, concerned that the couple might split and Marwan would lose his special 'Nasser effect', the Israelis purchased a diamond ring in Tel Aviv and Asherov asked Marwan to give it to Mona as a present.

But the Mossad could also be astonishingly unprofessional, putting Marwan in great danger of being exposed. They shared his information with the CIA, usually giving it to the CIA's director, Richard Helms, without properly concealing its source, and the CIA professionals easily detected that it came from Ashraf Marwan. On one occasion, a CIA official who knew Marwan, as Marwan often delivered messages from President Sadat directly to the CIA, confided to him that some information in CIA files 'surely comes from you'. Marwan was furious, and when he next saw Dubi Asherov he complained that the Mossad had failed to protect him properly.[7] Asherov apologized profusely, but this did not stop the Mossad from continuing to endanger their top spy; even while Marwan insisted that the circle of people who knew about him must remain as small as possible, the Mossad kept widening the circle. On one occasion, Asherov asked Marwan to meet an Israeli professor in chemical and biological warfare to discuss Egyptian chemical capabilities. Marwan was reluctant, but in the end he agreed on condition that the professor would not know his real identity. Two meetings were arranged but, at the end of the second one, when the professor departed he shook hands and said, 'See you, Mr Marwan.'[8]

———

While Marwan's trust in the Mossad was undermined, the Israelis' faith in him kept on increasing. They promoted him from being a provider of information to a 'warning' agent, whose main task would be to raise the alarm should an Egyptian attack on Israel become imminent. His handlers trained him to use a wireless transmitter, so that in case of danger of war he could send a quick message of warning that would be intercepted by an advanced receiver located at the Mossad's headquarters in Herzliya, just north of Tel Aviv. It was a bulky device with black pushbuttons, quite similar to the wireless communication set used by another spy, Eli Cohen, to send messages to Israel from Damascus, where he spied for the Israelis, but which had ended badly: the Syrians found the Israeli spy with the transmitter and hanged him in a Damascus square in 1965. Marwan did not like the gadget; if caught with it he would be in danger of being hanged like Cohen. So, politely, he accepted it, but back in Cairo he put the transmitter in a paper bag, walked down to the Nile and dropped the bag into the river.[9]

Yet, even without the electronic device at his disposal, Marwan raised the alarm at least twice, warning the Israelis of an imminent Egyptian attack. He did so first in November 1972 and then again in April 1973. For the Israelis, both warnings were confusing, as on the basis of Marwan's past information they only expected an Egyptian attack after certain preconditions were met, namely the arrival in Egypt of Soviet weaponry – and at the time of Marwan's warnings it was known in Israel that Egypt hadn't yet got that equipment. While in 1972 the Israelis did nothing with Marwan's warning, in April 1973, when Marwan warned them again of an imminent war, they decided not to take any chances and ordered a massive deployment of forces to counter a possible joint Egyptian and Syrian invasion, as indicated by Marwan. In fact, no attack came, neither in November 1972 nor in April 1973; and yet, despite these occasional errors, most of Marwan's information was accurate and jaw-dropping. One case in particular serves to illustrate his extraordinary value to Israel.

On 21 February 1973, a Libyan Boeing 727, flight number 114, en route from Benghazi to Cairo, was caught in a storm and started heading towards Israel. Concerned that it was flying to Dimona to crash into the nuclear reactor there, or perhaps even to Tel Aviv, the Israelis dispatched two aircraft which, failing to turn it back, opened fire and shot the plane down. It later emerged that because of a sand storm in the desert, the pilot of the Libyan aircraft had made a navigational error and, instead of flying in the direction of Egypt, headed towards Israel. All 105 passengers, including a former Libyan foreign minister, perished in the desert.

Libya's leader, the unpredictable Colonel Muammar Qaddafi, was furious, demanding that Egypt, whom he part-blamed for the crash, should retaliate against Israel. President Sadat attempted to calm the Colonel down by saying that Egypt's forces were preparing for a decisive battle against Israel which would be suitable revenge for the Libyan plane, as well as for many other Arab humiliations, and that it would be unwise to be distracted from the main battle by secondary incidents. Qaddafi remained unconvinced and vowed to take his revenge anyway. In a last-ditch attempt to dissuade Qaddafi from spoiling Egypt's careful plan to launch a surprise attack on Israel, Sadat travelled to Tripoli. But to no avail. Israel, Qaddafi insisted, must understand that Libya was not a soft touch and that there should be, in the tradition of the desert, an eye for an eye and a tooth for a tooth. Realizing the Libyan Colonel was adamant, Sadat asked him what sort of revenge he had in mind, to which Qaddafi replied that he wanted to blow up an Israeli El Al plane. Sadat then surprised Qaddafi by saying that Egypt could help. Then and there, he appointed his right-hand man, Ashraf Marwan, to liaise with Qaddafi over the delicate operation to hit an Israeli civilian aircraft. Subsequently, with one of Qaddafi's top agents, a Major Hawny, Marwan planned an operation. It was to take place in Rome where, as past experience showed, security was lax and, if anything went wrong, the authorities were known to be soft on captured terrorists. A team of five Palestinians, hand-picked by Colonel Qaddafi, would sneak up to the perimeter fence of Rome's international airport, then fire a portable missile at an Israeli jet as it took off.

The next step was taken by Marwan. He packed two missiles – supplied by the Egyptian army – into boxes for dispatch via Egypt's civilian airline to Rome. On them he wrote his wife's name, 'Mona Nasser', assuming that the Italians would not open boxes stamped with a diplomatic stamp and with the famous Nasser name printed on them. Mona – who did not know what the boxes contained – accompanied them on the flight to Rome. Marwan was right: the boxes passed through customs without a hitch and, in Rome, Mona handed the boxes over to Egyptian diplomatic personnel, who, as instructed, transferred them to the Egyptian Arts Academy in Rome. Upon receiving a message from his wife that the packages had arrived safely, Marwan boarded a flight to Italy. At a shoe shop, Raphael Salato, in central Rome he met the Palestinian leader of the group which would carry out the attack on the Israeli plane. A problem arose when it emerged that the Palestinian did not have a car to transport the missiles. So they bought some carpet from a nearby shop, rolled the missiles in it and carried the weapons on their backs to the underground train, from where they went to a flat in Ostia.[10]

When Marwan was finished, he picked up the phone, called Dubi Asherov and explained what had happened – adding where the missiles and Palestinian team could be found. The Mossad's director, Zvi Zamir, rushed to Rome to meet his Italian counterparts to explain the situation, but without revealing the name of his source. Subsequently, Italian police, just after midnight on 5 September 1973, launched their raid: they arrived at a house in Ostia, climbed to the second floor, knocked on the door of flat number 12, rounded up the occupants and confiscated the missiles. A few hours later, the rest of the Palestinian terrorist team arrived in Italy and were arrested at the small Atlas Hotel in central Rome.

Marwan's warning, no doubt, saved lives and with that his reputation within the Mossad soared even higher. A few weeks later, he provided the Israelis with what is still regarded as his most dramatic piece of information ever – in fact, information which the leading Israeli expert on the Yom Kippur War,

Uri Bar-Joseph, defines as 'the most important' intelligence Israel ever received.

———

From Paris on 4 October 1973 Marwan contacted his Mossad control, 'Alex'. This time he was careful not to phone the Israeli embassy directly; instead, he used the system by which he relayed a message through a lady in London, who then contacted the embassy with the code word for Asherov. Marwan's message was that Asherov should wait for him to phone again; upon receiving this message Asherov rushed to a safe flat, where he waited for Marwan's call. When they finally spoke Marwan was brief and to the point. He said that he wanted to discuss 'lots of chemicals' and to see in London on the next day the 'general' – a reference to Zvi Zamir, who was a former military general.

Marwan was a chemist by training, and many of the agreed emergency code words the Israelis equipped him with came from the world of chemistry, as he would more easily remember them. Moreover, to anyone listening on the line, Marwan mentioning chemical substances would not be suspicious, seeing as he was a chemist. 'Lots of chemicals' was an agreed code for a warning of war, a notice that Egypt intended to attack Israel from across the Suez Canal. However, 'lots of chemicals' was a general, not a specific warning of war; it was not the most serious of warnings. Should Marwan have wished to warn of an imminent or an immediate attack on Israel then he had in his arsenal specific codes to do so. But Marwan's request to see the director of the Mossad was unusual; true, they had met before in person, and Zamir, having such an important spy on his lists, had always been personally involved in handling him, but then all the previous meetings between Marwan and Zamir were initiated by the Mossad, not Marwan. But now, perhaps for the first time ever, it was Marwan who asked to see Zamir.

After putting down the phone Asherov summarized his conversation with Marwan, contacted the Mossad's headquarters in Tel Aviv and reported; he also summoned, upon Marwan's request, Zamir to London to meet the Egyptian. While Marwan's warning was not of an imminent attack on Israel, taken together with major Egyptian and Syrian movements of forces along the borders, which the Israelis had spotted but had done nothing about, it seemed to be more ominous. So Zamir boarded a private jet and hurried to the UK to meet his most senior spy; in the meantime, Marwan himself departed Paris for London and checked into a suite on the seventh floor of the Churchill Hotel, near Oxford Street.

———

FRIDAY, 5 OCTOBER, 10 P.M.
Zamir and Asherov wait for Marwan to arrive at the Mossad safe flat in Kensington, central London. The building is surrounded by ten armed agents, led by Zvi Malkin, an

experienced Mossad field commander, to protect the head of their organization, and if necessary to break in and rescue him.[11] As usual Marwan is late and there is a lot of tension in the air. Once again he seems to demonstrate an air of reckless-ness, as he arrives at the flat an hour and a half late, driven by a chauffeur in a car which belongs to the Egyptian em-bassy. Marwan has an explanation for his late arrival though. He says that he was held up at the Egyptian consulate in Kensington, where he tried to gather as much information as he could from Cairo.

Now Marwan goes straight to the heart of the matter: he has asked to see Zamir in person, he says, to issue him with a warning of an imminent attack on Israel, which will start in less than twenty-four hours, coordinated between Syria and Egypt. While Asherov takes notes Zamir listens atten-tively. Can he trust Marwan? Marwan is the most important spy in his organization, but twice before – the previous year and again just six months ago – he had warned of a war that never happened. And, today, there's a special problem: it is Yom Kippur, the Day of Atonement. Is Zamir prepared to rec-ommend to the government a full mobilization of the entire nation on the holiest day in the Jewish calendar to face an at-tack which might or might not happen? To instruct Israelis to abandon synagogues, break the fast, put on uniforms and rush to the front? Zamir asks questions and Marwan does his best to reassure him that war is indeed in the offing. He explains how Egyptian troops will cross the Suez Canal over five bridg-es, advance ten kilometres into the occupied Sinai and stop under their missile umbrella to protect them from Israeli air attacks; meanwhile, Syrian forces will strike in the north and invade the occupied Golan Heights. The time of attack, says Marwan: 6 October, at sunset. That's just a few hours away.

After nearly two hours the meeting is over; Mossad agents who follow Marwan can see that he returns to his hotel. Soon after, Zamir and Asherov emerge from the safe flat and hurry to the Israeli embassy. For Zamir this is an agonizing moment as he is fully aware of the ramifications of a massive mobilization of reserve soldiers on Yom Kippur. But he decides that he has no other choice, as to ignore the warning of war he has just received from the man he often describes as 'our best spy ever' would be irresponsible. So at 2.30 a.m. on 6 October, in a coded telephone call to Israel, Zamir sounds the alarm.

———

When the prime minister, Golda Meir, the defence minister, Moshe Dayan, and the Army Chief of Staff, David Elazar, met in Tel Aviv soon after they received the warning of an imminent war, they were divided and not sure what to do next. Dayan, who as the defence minister was directly responsible for the military, was reluctant to order a full mobilization, saying to the prime minister that on the basis of a warning from 'Zvi's friend [a reference to Marwan] you don't move everything to war'. But the prime minister sided with her military

Chief of Staff, who insisted that they should act on Marwan's warning and mobilize the entire nation – the reserve forces, tanks, artillery, planes, everything in fact – to face the coming attack. So in the middle of Yom Kippur, as a result of Marwan's London warning that war was to start soon, Israeli citizens in their thousands were called up: they abandoned synagogues, broke the fast, put on the uniforms which they kept at home and hurried to the front.

An Egyptian bridge over the Suez Canal, 6 October 1973. Marwan misled the Mossad about the time the Egyptians would attack across the canal

Unlike in 1972 and April 1973, this time Marwan was correct: Egypt and Syria did indeed launch a massive invasion. Thousands of Egyptian troops crossed the Suez Canal and planted flags inside the Israeli-occupied Sinai, and on the Golan Heights hundreds of Syrian tanks broke through the lines and easily overcame the few Israelis who defended the area, as the bulk of the army – the reserves – was still far away. But whereas Marwan's London warning was of a 'sunset' invasion, the actual attack came earlier, at two o'clock in the afternoon.

Part II

CHAPTER 4

I Unmask Marwan

———

MANY YEARS HAVE PASSED BUT the picture is still clear in my mind.

I am sitting at the kitchen table with my mum. She's having chicken soup but I am not. I am fasting. Not to eat and drink for a whole day is no easy matter for a fifteen-year-old, and it's just past two in the afternoon. It's Yom Kippur, 1973. Then someone is calling my mum's name from under our balcony. I can recognize the voice. It's Mazel, our next-door neighbour. Mum takes her plate with her and steps out onto the balcony. But it's not necessary as Mazel is quite excited. 'Turn the radio on … Turn the radio on,' she screams at the top of her voice. 'War has just broken out.'

So traumatic! So out of the blue! So unlike 1967, when our troops defeated Arab armies so quickly and elegantly. Back then, my dad woke me up one morning, pointing at a picture in a half-folded newspaper, telling me – a sleepy nine-year-old – that the man in the picture, Moshe Dayan, would soon lead us to a great victory over the Arabs. I remember looking at the picture and seeing someone with a black eye-patch who looked like a pirate; as a young boy I knew that pirates always win wars and I was happy enough. But now, six years on, the pirate is on our black-and-white TV screen, defeated, his head bowed and his voice trembling as he tells us that our troops at the front are fighting an invading enemy and that 'we are fighting for our lives!' Fighting for our lives? Us?

In subsequent years, the Yom Kippur trauma continued to deeply affect our collective life, as losing close to 3,000 young men touched upon every corner of the then small Israeli community. And as I grew up and moved from high school to army to university, and then turned my attention to the history of Israel's wars and even pen a few books on the subject, I realized that of all Israel's wars, it is the 1973 Yom Kippur War which is the most exciting: the story of a superb Arab surprise attack, which succeeds in catching Israel totally off balance, and an almost miraculous Israeli comeback and counter-attack which takes Israeli troops to the gates of Cairo and Damascus. But, above all, it's a John le Carré espionage drama, at the heart of which is a colourful superspy, whose name is shrouded in mystery and is top secret in Israel.

———

After issuing his warning to Zvi Zamir in London on 5 October 1973 that war would break out on the next day, Ashraf Marwan returned to Egypt. There he continued to work busily for President Sadat as a roving ambassador, delivering personal messages to Arab leaders to coordinate their moves in an attempt to take advantage of the successful surprise attack on Israel. But no sooner had the war ended than contact between Marwan and the Mossad resumed. Now the Mossad had a new request for Marwan – they wanted him to spy on Syria too. The Israeli concern was that the fragile ceasefire on the Golan Heights might collapse and Syria would resume the war. So Dubi Asherov, Marwan's case officer, sent him on espionage missions in Syria to find out what the Syrian intentions were on the Golan.

Marwan began work immediately. He travelled to Damascus to meet President Hafez al-Assad; the Syrian leader spoke openly with Marwan, and after the meeting Marwan contacted the Israelis. He had good news, and reported that President Assad did not intend to resume hostilities and would probably stick to the agreed ceasefire. Indeed, soon after, Israel and Syria signed further agreements that stabilized the ceasefire on the Golan. But Marwan did not neglect Egypt. At the same time as talks between Israel and Egypt took place in the Sinai desert to end hostilities, Marwan provided the Israelis with information that helped them gain the upper hand in the negotiations.

The crisis was over – and Israel, Egypt and Syria settled down to an uneasy peace. In Cairo, in the meantime, Marwan's star continued to rise. He was promoted from job to job in Anwar Sadat's administration and along the way – feared, mistrusted and disliked – he made himself many enemies; in Cairo he was dubbed 'Dr Death'. He also became a very rich man, as he was charged with Egypt's arms-purchasing programme and he earned himself substantial commissions through these arms deals, monies which went into his overseas bank accounts.

Wearing sunglasses, Ashraf Marwan came to be known in Cairo as "Dr Death"

At the same time, as relations between Israel and Egypt improved – the two countries signed a peace treaty in 1979 and Israel returned the occupied Sinai to Egypt – Marwan lost much of his importance as a spy for Israel. In fact, he became too much of a liability for the Israelis; if he had been caught spying for them now, it could seriously damage the peace between the two countries. So while the Israelis did not drop him, they rarely now called on him.

———

What happened next would change everything, both for Egypt and, once again, for Ashraf Marwan.

In 1981 President Anwar Sadat was assassinated by Islamic fundamentalists during a military parade in Egypt to commemorate what they regarded as the Egyptian victory over Israel in 1973. Sadat was succeeded by his vice-president, Hosni Mubarak. The new leader did not invite Marwan to join his inner circle, and that year Marwan left Cairo with his family. His destination was London, but on the way he stopped over in Paris and bought an expensive house, installing Mona and his children there before proceeding to the UK.

For Marwan, London was, of course, not a new place: he had been a student there, and most of his spying career for the Israelis had taken place there. But now he was financially secure; it is estimated he had between £300m and £500m in various accounts. At first, he lived in a comfortable house in Hampstead in north London, from where he would often emerge to be seen having a quiet whisky in a local pub, the Duke of Hamilton, while reading Arabic newspapers and the *Financial Times*. Soon after his arrival in the British capital, Marwan embarked on a spree of property purchasing; he began to build up a property and business empire, including part-ownership of Chelsea Football Club. He also became a full-time arms dealer, breaking UN sanctions and shipping weapons to Africa and elsewhere. This latter activity concerned Marwan's old paymaster – the Mossad – as the Israelis saw their spy developing a friendship with Libya's Colonel Qaddafi, a sworn enemy of Israel. When the Mossad began to suspect that Marwan was supplying Qaddafi with arms, they started spying on their old spy; they broke into his house to photocopy documents to try to establish whether he was trading arms with Libya, and installed secret cameras and listening devices in his home.

In the early 1980s, Marwan moved to London where he became a successful businessman

From London, Marwan kept close links with the Egyptian elite: one of his sons married the daughter of Amr Moussa, formerly the Egyptian foreign minister and then the secretary-general of the Arab League, while his other son, Gamal, was a close friend and business partner of Gamal Mubarak, son of President Mubarak. By the early 1980s, Marwan's contacts with the Mossad had dwindled to almost nothing – save for one occasion when he found himself in a sudden financial crisis and turned to them for help; he was then paid a lump sum of half a million dollars in lieu of the years he had worked for no money. It would be the last time the Mossad paid him.

————

There is a coda – and it marks the end of Marwan's spying career for the Israelis.

In the mid-1990s the Mossad decided to revive the dormant relationship with Marwan, as the Israelis recognized that Marwan's web of contacts across the Middle East and beyond could benefit them. So 'Alex' – Dubi Asherov, Marwan's old case officer – was sent to London to renew the contact.

From the day he joined the Mossad in 1970, Marwan insisted on two conditions: first, that only 'Alex' would handle him; and second, that he would never be secretly or otherwise recorded. His first request was fulfilled, as the Mossad allowed – albeit reluctantly – Asherov to remain Marwan's sole control, which he was for twenty-eight years until the end of Marwan's work with the Mossad. The second request was never actually fulfilled, as in the apartment where most meetings with Marwan took place, near the Dorchester Hotel, the Mossad installed secret recording systems; but at least Marwan did not know about it.[1] Now, however, the new director of the Mossad, Danny Yatom, concerned about the too-close Asherov–Marwan relationship and wanting to know what passed between them, ruled that Asherov should carry a tape recorder in his pocket and record his conversation with Marwan.[2]

Asherov and Marwan met over dinner and things started well; the two men were delighted to see each other again as they had gone through so much together. But then disaster struck; when Asherov's hidden tape recorder reached the end, a mechanism fault caused it to start playing the recorded conversation aloud. Embarrassed, Asherov hurried to the bathroom to silence the machine, leaving a deeply offended Marwan at the table. When Asherov returned he apologized profusely, but he was experienced enough to know that it was a disastrous mishap. Indeed, this turned out to be the last ever meeting between Marwan and Asherov. Betrayed and hurt, Marwan refused to meet anyone from the Mossad again. The next Israeli Marwan had a relationship with was not a Mossad operator, but an academic – myself.

———

Like other scholars of Israel's wars I, too, knew that once upon a time there was a 'miraculous' Arab spy who had worked for the Mossad before the Yom Kippur War and went on to provide a critical warning of war. In my early works on Israel's wars I had hardly ever mentioned him as I had so little to add. It all changed in 1998 when I interviewed Eli Zeira for a BBC TV documentary series called *The Fifty Years War: Israel and the Arabs*.

Zeira is a well-known figure in Israel – an intelligent and charismatic retired military general who participated in Israel's wars from 1948. In the lead-up to the 1973 Yom Kippur War he served as the director of the Military Intelligence directorate (AMAN, in Hebrew) – it was his job to advise the prime minister and the government as a whole on the probability of war with the Arabs breaking out.

In the Israel of the 1970s, Eli Zeira was a rising star who, it was often thought, would one day become chief of staff of the Army and perhaps even go on to be a leading political figure. But the problem with Zeira was that he was too confident and arrogant – not the best characteristics for a director of Military Intelligence, who must be a good listener and, above all, cautious – even hesitant – with his analyses and advice, as they carry so much weight and responsibility. In the months before the Yom Kippur War Zeira's over-confidence led him – and as a consequence led the prime minister and her government – to believe that the Arabs would not dare to attack Israel, and that the chance of war breaking out was, as Zeira put it to the prime minister, Golda Meir, 'lower than low' – war, he believed, was an impossibility. But Zeira was wrong, as Egypt and Syria did attack and caught Israel almost totally unprepared.

Director of Military Intelligence during the 1973 Yom Kippur war, Israeli General Eli Zeira, suspected that Ashraf Marwan was a double agent

When the war was over and the true price of it was revealed –
not only in money but also in blood – the public was enraged
and soon heads started rolling, the first one being Zeira's. A
National Inquiry commission, headed by the Supreme Court's
Chief Justice Shimon Agranat, pointed the finger at Zeira, blam-
ing him for stubbornly clinging to a false idea that there would
be no war, blinding Israel's leaders to an attack until it was nearly
too late. Zeira was depicted as the ultimate villain and the chief
person responsible for the Yom Kippur disaster. Humiliated, he
resigned. The few friends who still met with him in his house in
north Tel Aviv reported that he was a broken man.

In subsequent years Zeira kept a low profile, keeping himself to himself and rejecting all invitations to comment on the
Yom Kippur War. He was still young, only forty-five, and full
of energy and intelligence, which he channelled into a successful business career. At the same time, he was privately working
on his memoirs, and when *Yom Kippur War: Myth vs. Reality*
was published, he started spearheading an aggressive campaign to clear himself of the Yom Kippur stain and to show
that the disaster was not his fault.

What Zeira claimed was intriguing: that while his responsibility as director of Military Intelligence was indeed
to advise the government on the probability of war with the
Arabs, and that his view was that the chance of an attack on
Israel was very low, the prime minister herself had the opportunity to overrule him, particularly as a secret and highly
placed visitor had come to see her just ten days before the
war to warn her of an imminent Arab invasion. Golda Meir,

Zeira said, chose to ignore the visitor's warning, so why blame Zeira for the failure? Who was the mysterious visitor who tipped off Meir? There had been rumours in Israel after the war that it was none other than King Hussein of Jordan who flew his helicopter to Tel Aviv to meet Golda Meir in person to inform her, and he did so because he was afraid that if war broke out there would be pressure on him in the Arab world to join the fight against Israel, which he was reluctant to do. But there was no proof to substantiate these rumours.

Now, in 1998, when my BBC interview was finished, Zeira said, without being asked, that he could give me the 'smoking gun' to show that it had indeed been King Hussein who advised Golda Meir of the impending war. Zeira, I immediately registered, wanted to use me to provide the proof that the king had warned her and that Meir had ignored him, and she could equally have ignored Zeira's view that there would be no war, and so it was *her* fault that Israel was not prepared for the attack. I was happy to be exploited by Zeira as it could land me with an amazing scoop, and I keenly accepted his invitation to drop by later in the evening to see the actual transcript of the conversation between King Hussein and Golda Meir and copy it down. Zeira was a little concerned that he would be revealed as my source and that this could land him in trouble, as the transcript of the conversation between the king and the prime minister was a top secret document which had never before been published. So I came up with the idea that instead of me getting the document directly from him, I would send my assistant, Nava

Mizrachi, to take down the relevant paragraphs. This way, I reassured Zeira, I could say that he did not give me the document and that I got it from someone else; this would not be a lie, merely a manipulation of the facts.

Here is King Hussein's warning of war as given by him to the prime minister, and published in my book *The Fifty Years War* in 1998 for the first time:

> King Hussein: ... from a very very sensitive source in Syria that we have received information from in the past and passed it on[3] ... all the [Syrian] units that are meant to be in training are now, as of the last two days or so, in position for a pre-attack ... in pre-jump positions [to attack Israel].
> Golda Meir: ... is it conceivable that the Syrians would start something without the full cooperation of the Egyptians?
> King Hussein: I don't think so. I think they would cooperate.

But that was not all. As we stood there in Zeira's kitchen, leaning against the wall chatting, negotiating how I would get the Hussein document from him without revealing him as my source, Zeira uttered a '*Ze klum*', meaning 'that's nothing' in Hebrew. '*Ha'sipur Ha'amiti*' – 'the real story' – he continued, is that the Mossad were 'misled by an untrustworthy Egyptian double agent'. I tried to push my luck and see if he would provide me with more information about the mysterious 'double agent'. But here Zeira was careful and unwilling to play ball – he moved his hand in a zipping movement across his mouth to imply that he was not going to add a thing.

———

In subsequent weeks I became ever more interested in this 1973 spy story – obsessed is a better word to describe it – and did all I could to crack the nut and find out who the mysterious spy was and whether he was a genuine spy working for Israel, or – as Zeira claimed – a Trojan horse, an agent planted in the Mossad to deceive and ultimately betray them. I collected each and every scrap of information, of which there was not much, read all that was to be read on the Yom Kippur War, and made lists of 'potential' spies. As I pored over the documents and memoirs I drew up a shortlist of three potential spies, which I faxed to Zeira. His reply came in the shape of a short and abrupt fax message: 'You'll learn nothing from me!' So I continued fumbling, but bit by bit I managed to delete names from my 'potential spies' list until I was left with a single name – Ashraf Marwan, the son-in-law of President Gamal Abdel Nasser, who became my white whale. My next step would get me even closer to solving the mystery.

Zeira, as I have mentioned earlier, published his memoirs back in the early 1990s, when he wrote of – though stopped short of naming – the Egyptian 'double agent'. Zeira was clearly not prepared to help me with the matter – but there was someone who might. Rami Tal was Zeira's editor – and he was someone I knew. It might be, I calculated, that the two discussed the name. So I flew to Israel, phoned Tal and invited him for a drink. I had planned my meeting with him meticulously and rehearsed it carefully, knowing that I'd probably got one chance and should I fail I'd be stuck for a long time. I ran through what *exactly* I would say to Tal, where *exactly* I would drop the name 'Ashraf Marwan' into the course of our conversation, and what *exactly* I would look at when mentioning the name. My plan was to try and see if Tal's body language confirmed that Ashraf Marwan was the mysterious spy.

We met at Beit Sokolov, a popular Tel Aviv meeting place for journalists, and we sipped horrible weak and lukewarm coffee from plastic cups. Then, as I had planned in advance, ten minutes or so into our conversation, when Tal was warmed up but not yet tired of me, I said, out of the blue, 'Ashraf Marwan's the man', and I looked straight into Tal's eyes. His response was unmistakable, he looked away and smiled; Tal's body language confirmed to me that Ashraf Marwan was the top Egyptian Mossad spy.

I returned to London excited and euphoric, as I knew I had managed, after months of investigation, to crack the nut. But I also knew that I had to tread carefully; the evidence was not yet strong enough. And what if I had got it wrong? What if Tal reacted in the way he did because of something else, not in reaction to me dropping Marwan's name? Such things, after all, are often in the eye of the beholder. So I took it step by step, and very carefully started to drop hints about the identity of Marwan, leaving myself just enough room to be able to withdraw should Marwan deny it, or if he threatened libel action. My plan was to raise the bar gradually, notch by notch, to try and elicit a response from him; should his reaction be too strong I would then have made a quick retreat and have forgotten about the business altogether, which in many ways would have been a relief.

I dropped my first hint in a chapter I wrote on the Yom Kippur War for my book *Israel's Wars*, published in 2000. There, I described a senior Egyptian who was, as I put it elliptically, 'the right-hand man' of Egypt's President Anwar Sadat, but who also served as a Mossad spy.[4] I embraced Eli Zeira's double-agent theory and explained that this person, whose name was still top secret, was actually a double agent, serving Egypt at a time when Israel considered him a super-spy on her behalf. By that time, with Marwan's name known to me – or at least I *thought* that he was the man – I also saw that Zeira's claim about Marwan playing a double game was not unreasonable.

There was the fact that he was a 'walk-in': he offered his services to the Mossad in 1970 unprompted, rather than being selected and recruited by them; thus he was clearly potentially a Trojan horse, planted by Egyptian intelligence to mislead. The testimonies of Mossad agents who followed Marwan's movements in London before and after meeting his case officer, Dubi Asherov, also, I thought, strengthened the double-agent theory. His confidence, after all, was quite astonishing, phoning the Israeli embassy directly, walking into meetings with Asherov without so much as glancing over his shoulder, and carrying top secret original documents in a bag to give to the Israelis. This could be seen as recklessness – and in later years, as I came to know Marwan personally, I detected this streak in his character – or else perhaps as confidence that he was safe meeting the Israelis, knowing that he was really there on Egypt's behalf. Zvi Malkin, an experienced Mossad operator who was often in charge of securing the meetings between Marwan and Asherov and with Zvi Zamir, the Mossad's director, and who often followed Marwan in London – and as far as Paris – to see with whom he met, testified as to how astonished he had always been at Marwan's behaviour. 'I saw him driving around with the registration number of the Egyptian embassy,' Malkin recalled, 'and this is how he came to see us [Mossad], with no fear, without any security precautions. I saw him enjoying himself in Paris in the Hotel George V with Sadat's wife Jihan and her daughter and did not trust him from the first moment … he was part of Sadat's deception [plan against Israel].'[5] Rafi Meidan, the head of the Mossad station in London, to whom Dubi Asherov, Marwan's direct controller, would report, also suspected that Marwan was misleading the Israelis. The British MI5, according to Meidan, was likely to know about the spying activities in the capital and it knew of Marwan and probably followed his moves, and it could have leaked to the Egyptians news about Marwan's meetings with the Israelis. But, according to Meidan, Marwan probably felt safe as he was sent to the meetings by the Egyptians in order to mislead the Israelis.[6]

And there were other indications to show that Marwan might have been a double agent. He, as shown, provided Israel with the data that would become the foundation of their 'Conception', the view developed in Israel before the Yom Kippur War that obtaining certain weapons – Scud missiles and long-range bombers – was an absolute precondition for Egypt before embarking on war against Israel. But when President Sadat realized that the Soviets would not provide him with these weapons, he decided to embark on a limited war against Israel anyway, without waiting for the weapons. Marwan, who must have known about this change as he was Sadat's right-hand man, failed to notify the Mossad. He thus left them clinging to a strategy – 'The Conception' – which was no longer valid and which led them to neglect any contradictory information showing that war was on their doorstep.[7]

What further strengthened my view that Marwan was misleading Israel was that twice before the war, in the autumn of 1972 and spring of 1973, as I have shown earlier, he warned the Israelis that Egypt would embark on war, but in both cases war failed to materialize. The warnings, particularly in April 1973, led to major preparations and mobilization of forces in Israel, and the maintenance of a high state of alert before the units were eventually dispersed. Marwan might have provided those false warnings in a sort of 'cry-wolf syndrome', or to enable the Egyptians to monitor how Israel reacted in such emergency situations, recasting their own military plans accordingly. The most incredible fact, however, concerned the date at which Egypt decided on war. In the memoirs of Egyptian officials of the period it is mentioned that the first time a firm decision to embark on war against Israel was actually taken was in Alexandria on 23 August 1973.[8] So how could Marwan tell the Mossad that it would happen in 1972 and in April 1973, *before* the decision had even been made in Egypt? And why, when on 28 August 1973 Sadat sat down with the Saudi king and told him that war against Israel would happen 'soon, very soon', did Marwan, who had been in the room with Sadat and the king – in fact, he was the only person with them in the room – report to the Israelis that Egypt had *delayed* plans for war? Why else if not to deceive them? Zeira, who was the person who had kindled in me the interest in Marwan in the first place, and in the idea that Marwan was misleading the Israelis, wrote in his memoirs that the fact that Marwan (unnamed by Zeira) concealed crucial information by failing to report this meeting to the Israelis shows that he was 'the jewel in the crown of the Egyptian deception plan'.[9]

Finally, the warnings which Marwan gave the Israelis on the eve of the war, just hours before it started, increased my suspicion that he might have misled his handlers. Surely, he must have known that the information he had provided the Mossad with did not allow Israel enough time to mobilize her forces to the fronts. And when he phoned Dubi Asherov from Paris he said he wanted to talk about 'lots of chemicals', a code to warn Israel of a general, non-specific danger of war. Marwan had much more specific code words that he could have used, thus giving the Israelis more time to mobilize.

Instead, Marwan summoned the director of the Mossad, Zvi Zamir, all the way to London to meet him the next day in order to whisper in his ear the specific warning of war. That meant another twenty-four hours' delay. And even when providing this late warning to Zamir it seems that Marwan was misleading him again, for his warning was that war would start at 'sunset' whereas in reality it began at two o'clock in the afternoon. The Israelis, wanting to act on Marwan's information but, at the same time, wary of revealing that they had advance knowledge of the attack, had planned to move their tanks into front-line positions at 4 p.m. But by 4 p.m. on 6 October it was much too late, as their positions had already been overrun by the invading enemy.

——————

From one of my students, an Egyptian who knew the Marwans, I got hold of Ashraf Marwan's London address. I put a copy of my new book, where I hint that he was a Mossad spy and double agent, in an envelope, having marked the relevant pages, and dedicated the book: 'To Ashraf Marwan, Hero of Egypt'. I sent it registered delivery, so that I would know he had received it, and left all my details there for him to be able to contact me if he decided to do so – my telephone number and home address. I then waited anxiously for him to react – but there was nothing. No response.

Two years went past; I published another book, *A History of Israel*. I decided I'd nothing to lose and so in this book I raised the bar – not by a notch, but quite dramatically. In a chapter on the Yom Kippur War, without spelling out his name, I wrote about the mysterious Mossad spy, and said that he was 'a very close family member of Egypt's President Nasser' and that in Israel he was dubbed 'The Son-in-Law'.[10] It was a lie, designed to provoke Marwan. Of course, it did not take a genius to surmise that the spy was Ashraf Marwan, but I still left myself an exit, just in case he overreacted. If he did, I decided, I would say in my defence that the Israelis used 'son-in-law' as a nickname for a spy, and one should not regard it as a description of his family status. As I did with *Israel's Wars*, I sent Marwan a copy of my book, bearing the inscription 'To Ashraf Marwan, Hero of Egypt', dispatching it to his London address by registered post. I waited anxiously for his response. Again nothing. Then – a dramatic development.

On 2 December 2002, the Egyptian newspaper *Sawt al-Ummah* asked Ashraf Marwan to answer the question – was he the person at the heart of my story? How a copy of my book got to them I had no idea. But what Marwan said to them was that my book was 'a stupid detective story'. In a childish sort of way I felt hurt and upset with Marwan's response and took it quite personally. But I also felt that he had blinked first; I expected him to say that he would take me to court for libel, but he did not, and the fact that he did not threaten legal action was interpreted by me as a weakness and as a final confirmation – indeed, an admission – that he was the spy. So when an Egyptian journalist from the *Al Ahram al Arabi* newspaper phoned from Cairo, asking for my response to Ashraf Marwan's rebuttal, I invited her to come and see me in London.

We sat in Starbucks in Wimbledon and she told me that her name was Halud el Gamal. She dug out a list of questions she wanted to ask me, which I ignored before proceeding to say what I wanted to say. I confirmed that the person I referred to as the 'Son-in-Law' in my book was indeed Ashraf Marwan, the son-in-law of President Nasser. Noting Marwan's dismissive remark regarding my claims as being 'a silly detective story', I said to Halud that I had to defend my good name as a historian and that I could not accept Marwan's allegations. I added that Ashraf Marwan was a perfect spy and an Egyptian national hero, who very successfully managed to trick Israel, and that he was the person who more than anyone else should be credited with Egypt's success in deceiving Israel before the 1973 Yom Kippur War, and that the Egyptians should name a street after him.[11]

After the interview I went straight home. I was calm and focused. It took me no more than a few inquiries to locate Marwan's offices in Cairo, where I assumed there was a fax machine. I talked to his secretary and, without giving away much, explained the urgency of the situation, whereupon she gave me Marwan's private fax number, to where I sent the following, which was my first ever communication with Marwan:

> To private fax AM: 00 202 4180423
> **Private and confidential**
> 9 December 2002
> Dear Ashraf (if I may),
>
> I was very disappointed with your interview for *Sawt al-Ummah* where you said that the story about the Son-in-Law in my book *A History of Israel* is a 'stupid detective story' (I don't myself read Arabic, and this is how your words were translated to me by a journalist from *Al Ahram*, who came to ask for my response to your allegations). Let me tell you just that: the story about the Son-in-Law was bound to be published – it was just a matter of time … If you wish to comment on my work you are more than welcome [to do so] and I am pretty sure you know how to contact me directly [given that I had left all my details in the books I'd sent him], but there is no point in challenging me over the pages of *Sawt al-Ummah*, thus forcing me to defend my reputation by responding to your allegations over the pages of *Al Ahram al Arabi*.

This was my way to explain to Marwan the motives behind the interview and, more importantly, to give him some time to prepare a counter-attack. I knew the revelations would have shocked him a great deal, for surely it is the greatest fear of a spy to wake up one morning to read his real name in the newspaper. He might also have wanted to take some precautions, maybe leave Egypt, or destroy documents which might have incriminated him; or he might have just wanted to have some time to perhaps talk about the matter to his wife and children.

————

A couple of weeks later, I took my wife and kids to Bayswater, a district in London with a large Arab population – and where newspapers and magazines are sold. I picked up a copy of *Al Ahram al Arabi* and over a Mediterranean lunch I leafed through the pages. I could detect the interview as my picture was there, as well as some of Marwan with Mona Nasser and her father. When the waiter arrived and I saw that he was of a Mediterranean background, I asked him to translate the headline. He read: 'ASHRAF MARWAN A PERFECT SPY AND NATIONAL HERO'; that was an actual quote from the interview I gave. I shivered. The revelation would no doubt cause a sensation in the Arab world, where Marwan was well known on account of his marriage to Mona Nasser, and of course in the Mossad. And how would the Mossad react to my claims that Marwan misled them? How would they respond to the unmasking of what they considered to be their top spy ever? We left the restaurant and strolled in nearby Hyde Park, but my thoughts were elsewhere, so I left my family there and returned home, where I sat at my desk to write a letter to Marwan; I faxed it to his Cairo private fax machine:

Private and confidential
29 December 2002
Dear Ashraf (if I may),

I have here a copy of *Al Ahram Al Arabi* (21 December 2002) with my interview about the Son-in-Law. I can't read Arabic but I do hope that this piece reflects what was said in the interview. What is clear to me though – given all the photographs which ac-company the interview – is that the name of the Son-in-Law is clearly spelled out ...

CHAPTER 5

Our Relationship

———

30 December 2002

It is cold and wet, and I am in the garden, wearing my boots and sweeping the fallen leaves. My wife is in the kitchen cooking and through the steam I can see her banging on the French windows with her fist while holding her right hand to her ear to signal that someone is on the line for me. I walk inside, lift the receiver and say 'Hello', to which the person at the other end of the line says through a thick Arabic accent: 'How are you?' I frown, trying to recognize the voice. 'I am fine,' I finally say, 'and who is this?' 'I am the man you've written about,' he replies. I am taken aback. Is it *really* Ashraf Marwan on the line, or is it a prank? 'And how can I be sure you are who you say you are?' I reply. The voice says, simply: 'You've sent me the book with the dedication.'

This is the first time we speak to each other and we both struggle to carry the conversation away from our too often repeated 'How are you?' He complains that he is ill ('just had three major operations') before he turns to what sounds to me like a well-rehearsed little speech. 'Listen,' he launches, 'I want to say three more things to you: first, I am not challenging you [regarding my claims that he was a double agent working for Egypt]. Second, you have your enemies and I have mine – don't listen to my enemies. Third, we should meet up when I am better ... *but don't listen to my enemies.*' He clearly suspects that his so-called 'enemies', perhaps journalists, are trying to drive a wedge between us and squeeze from each of us statements that make up good newspaper stories. He also, quite clearly, wants the entire affair to calm down. A long silence! We have so much to say to each other, but it feels as if we both cannot put it all into words. So, wishing each other (one a Jew, the other a Muslim) Merry Christmas, we end the conversation and ring off.

————

We began a stuttering relationship, mainly short exchanges on the phone; and often, when I put the phone down, I felt as if he was just calling me to check that I was still there and that I was not going to do any more silly things that could hurt him. He was always polite, always asking about the family – my children, my wife, about my projects – speaking slowly and deliberately in broken English.

And the more he phoned and the more he showed interest and asked personal questions, the more I became concerned for him. For as long as he had been a distant spy with no face –

'the Son-in-Law', 'the Angel', 'the source' – I did not care
much about him as a human being, but now that I could hear
his voice, him breathing heavily on the other end of the line,
learned about his health problems, the operations, the pains,
his sons ('don't speak to them'), then the spy was no longer a
spy, but he was real, an ordinary mortal – 'Ashraf' I called him,
his first name. I spent sleepless nights, deeply concerned that
something might happen to him; that perhaps the Egyptians
might not buy my story about him being their national hero,
their double agent who misled the Israelis, and hurt him. Or
that the Mossad might do something stupid. Or both: that the
Mossad, in an attempt to show that rather than being a double
agent Marwan was a genuine spy, might release incriminat-
ing information about him, and that the Egyptians, acting
on this information, might exact their revenge on Marwan
for betraying them. So, ironically, from trying to uncover this
most important spy in Middle Eastern espionage history, I
now shifted to trying to protect him; constantly – obsessively,
as is often the case with me – keeping an eye on any relevant
piece of information which might affect his safety and reporting it to him. My work: the writing, teaching, family – all was
put aside.

We developed a sort of unofficial working relationship
conducted through Marwan's Cairo office, where his private
secretary, Oweida – or perhaps Gaza was her name – was in
charge of his private fax machine, which Marwan instructed
me to continue using, as I had hitherto, in order to contact
him. The process was quite simple: I would phone Marwan's

secretary from London and alert her that I was about to send
a fax. A minute or so later I would send my message and she'd
collect it at the other end and somehow deliver it to Marwan
or, if he was abroad, forward it to him. The messages I sent him
were mainly about items written on him in the Israeli press,
or elsewhere, which I thought might affect his safety. He always got back to me promptly, even if the information did not
require any immediate response, often within a few moments
of me sending the fax. He was intuitive and he recognized my
growing guilt about unmasking him and my concern about
his safety, and I often felt that he was taking advantage of it.

From my diary; part of a message I sent to Marwan:

22 January 2003
Dear Ashraf,
    I was very sad to hear, when we last talked, that
you are unwell and I do very much hope that you feel
better now. After more than four years of work on this
story, I feel that I know you quite well and I sympa-
thize with you very much and feel quite guilty that the
publication of my book, and in particular the follow-
up interview with *al Ahram*, came at a most inconve-
nient time for you …

Marwan had strange habits, those of a real spy. He would
phone and keep quiet, just listening to my voice on the other end of the line; I sometimes heard him breathing on the

other side. He would then put down the phone and ring me again and start a conversation. He identified himself but he very rarely used his real name. He would say, 'This is your friend', or 'This is the person you've written about' or 'This is about the book'. He was always polite, but behind his politeness I also sensed a certain distance, impatience, toughness, perhaps even anger. 'The ruthless good manners of a spy,' I often thought to myself.

From my diary (a copy of a fax I sent to Marwan):

Private & Confidential
12 February 2003
Dear Ashraf,

I hope my letter finds you in good health and that you feel much better now. Why am I writing again? To say that my literary agent is now in talks with publishers in America to secure me a contract to write a full length book on the Son-in-Law ... will you cooperate with me (confidentially) on this project? Will you tell me your side of the story? I can see two main reasons why you might want to do so: 1. Somewhere in the future books on this story will be published. So why not do it now and with me ... and thus ensure that the Son-in-Law is portrayed in the best possible light and as a hero of Egypt? 2. In return for cooperating with me I'll allow you almost full control over the list of people I intend to interview and then let you see and comment on the final product before publication.

I can't, I am afraid, guarantee you full control over the material ... but I'll try my best – and that's a lot – to always take your views on board.

Let me be honest and make it crystal clear; my decision whether or not to go ahead with this book is not dependent on your cooperation or non-cooperation ... I <u>do not</u> want to upset you, Ashraf, and I'll listen very attentively to reservations you have – if any. But I do hope that you will agree to help in this project, which I strongly believe is in your interest, and with your help will secure the good reputation of the Nasser–Marwan family for many generations to come.

In the meantime, an American producer from CBS's flagship show *60 Minutes* kept nagging me about a TV programme he was producing on Ashraf Marwan. I thought it was a unique opportunity to give a big push to the Marwan double-agent story and so I sent a message to Marwan to contact me.

From my diary (a summary of a telephone conversation with Marwan):

6 June 2003
Ashraf Marwan phoned today at 11.22. Conversation lasted some fifteen minutes. He talked from a cab (according to him) obviously in London. The following is based on notes taken during the conversation:
AM: 'Dr Bregman?'

AB: 'Yes, who's calling?'

AM: 'Ahron?'

AB: 'Yes, speaking. And who are you?'

AM: 'I received your fax [in which I had asked to talk to him to discuss *60 Minutes*.]'

AB: 'How are you?'

AM: 'I am sick … some complications …'

AB: 'Oh dear! Have you been contacted by the American author?'

AM: 'What American?'

AB: 'Howard … Howard Blum.'

AM: 'What's his name again?'

AB: 'Howard Blum … They do a television programme to promote his book … *60 Minutes* … have they approached you?'

AM: 'No.'

AB: 'Will you participate if they do?'

AM: 'No.'

AB: 'Why not?'

AM: 'I want [this story] to die …'

AB: 'It will not …'

[Marwan now switches the conversation to talk about the Mossad, who, he believes, are orchestrating an entire campaign against him.]

AM: 'Why do they [Mossad] want to take this revenge?'

AB: 'It's not revenge …'

AB: 'Will you appear on the show?'

AM: 'No … I'll have to contradict you [if he appears, and say that he didn't spy].'

AB: 'I am not asking for your permission … but what would be your view if I decided to appear on the show?'

AM: 'Yes, it's OK … you can do it … you go …'

AB: 'I am writing a book on the Son-in-Law … I need your help …'

AM: 'I'll sort out my health first and then we'll meet … but don't talk to them … to the Egyptians …'

AB: 'OK … best of luck …'

AM: 'To you too.'

———

20 OCTOBER 2003

It is quite early in the morning and I am at my desk, still in my pyjamas. The phone rings but when I pick it up there is no one at the other end. It is, of course, Ashraf Marwan, using one of his telephone etiquettes. So I grab my notebook and am ready with pen in hand to take notes of our conversation. Since our first telephone chat the year before, I meticulously record our significant conversations, as I realize that I am now a participant in a bizarre story. 'It's your friend,' he says when I pick up again and he then proceeds through his normal routine, asking about family – wife, kids, schools, projects. He then launches into the matter at hand, the bottom line of which is an invitation to meet up face to face in London in ten days' time.

Three days later he surprises me when he phones to ask, 'What are you doing today?' I say that I am working from home, whereupon he suggests that I come into town and meet him at one o'clock at the Dorchester Hotel in Park Lane. I immediately say that I would rather meet elsewhere, for although I have never had proper espionage training, it just makes sense to try and mess up a little bit the plans of someone who might – just might – want to set a trap for you. Also, for Israelis who know a bit of history, the Dorchester has a terrible reputation: on 3 June 1982, three Palestinians attempted to assassinate the Israeli ambassador, which then triggered the Israeli invasion of Lebanon in which I myself participated as a young artillery officer. I can sense that Marwan is quite taken aback by my wish to change the venue, but he agrees to my suggestion that we have our rendezvous at the Intercontinental Hotel – it's not far from the Dorchester and I know the place quite well, as that is where I often meet Eli Zeira, the former director of Military Intelligence, for lunch.

It's quite late in the morning already so I quickly put on my best suit, as I know that, being an Egyptian, Marwan will be well dressed, and I scribble a note to my wife – she knows nothing about my espionage games – to say: 'Meeting with the Egyptian Ashraf Marwan at the Intercontinental Hotel, at 1 p.m.' I put the note on my desk so it is visible, and so that someone would know my whereabouts if Marwan did plan to harm me. I know I am playing with fire. I am about to meet up with a person whose nickname in Egypt in the 1970s was 'Dr Death'; who worked, or is still working, for the Mossad as well as for the CIA, MI6, the Italian security services and perhaps other agencies too; and he has all the reasons in the world to seek revenge after I have publicly unmasked him as a spy and probably ruined his life. I have always been a most responsible person, but there has also always been in me a reckless streak, just like in Marwan. I am not frightened, far from it, but I am very alert and I take some basic precautions.

At Wimbledon I board the train to Waterloo and from there jump on the London Underground in the direction of Park Lane, getting off one stop before where I would be expected to leave the train to go to the Intercontinental. I surface from the Underground and I head to the hotel through small side streets, stopping from time to time to check if I am being tailed. Nothing. When I reach the hotel I can see from a distance that someone is standing by the main entrance, bag on his back; so I cross to the other side of the street and then sneak in through a side entrance; as I said, I know the place quite well. I am a bit late and Marwan is already there. He is tall and slim, a good-looking man. As expected he is well dressed in an expensive suit with a red scarf round his neck. He is pacing backwards and forwards, looking at his mobile. 'Ashraf,' I say. He turns to me and smiles; we shake hands and he leads me to a deserted part of the lobby.

He orders coffees and when they do not come he gets up and fetches them for us. He's very polite, going through his usual enquiries about kids, schools, wife, work; very accommodating, charming, smiling, nodding, but also as nervous as me. When I fumble distractedly with my tie pin, he looks at my fingers, probably wondering whether I am filming or recording him. From my bag, I fish out some newspapers and spread them on the low coffee table which is in front of us, pointing at pictures of Zvi Zamir, director of the Mossad in 1973; Marwan looks intently at the picture, trying to identify the not-young-face of a person whom he had met quite often some thirty years before, not far from where we are sitting now. I want to talk to him about the book I am planning to write about him and that I need his assistance with. But, as always, he is full of surprises. He tells me that *he* is writing a book – a memoir – and that he wishes me to act as his consultant. 'I'll consult you from time to time,' he says. I am taken aback, but immediately say that if that's the case then there is no point in me writing his story too, and that I would be happy to help him. I ask him about Egypt and how the Egyptians have reacted to the revelations about his past. 'In Egypt,' he says curtly, 'we don't talk about this.' I try a direct question about his activities. I ask him about the warning he gave to the Israelis that war would start in the evening when, in fact, it started at two in the afternoon. Did he say so on purpose in order to mislead the Israelis? He smiles, he is a bit evasive and he finally speaks: 'A few hours ... does it really matter?' 'You're a colourful person,' I say, which he takes as a compliment and, beaming contentedly, he replies, 'Thank you.'

We finish our coffees, I gather up my papers and we stay a little bit longer before departing together. We walk to the front door and it is then, Marwan on my right, that he says that he is concerned that he might be assassinated. I turn to him and hasten to say that it is not in the interest of the Mossad to kill him, as this would cause more damage than good; it might deter potential spies from joining them. 'But I don't know about Egypt,' I add frankly. He does not reply, but he warns me not to contact his Cairo office any more as 'the Egyptians are monitoring it'. And not to phone his home number, 'as the British are monitoring it'. He gives me his mobile number and asks me to text him directly if necessary. A black car is waiting outside for him, the driver standing by its door. We shake hands again and we go our different ways. I return home, remove the note I've left for my wife, and sit down to summarize the meeting. What a day!

———

Marwan had warned me not to contact him in Cairo, but I might have had to do so regardless the following year, as I was to travel to Israel with a BBC crew to work on a TV documentary and was concerned that when I landed in Israel the authorities there might arrest me for revealing the name of a top Mossad spy. But who could rescue me if I was detained there? Ironically, I concluded, it could be Ashraf Marwan. He kept telling me that he wanted the entire story about him 'to die', but clearly if I were to be detained upon landing, especially travelling with a group of BBC journalists, such an arrest would make headlines. So, in case I was arrested, I prepared a letter which I deposited with my wife and which was to be faxed to Marwan's private fax in Cairo in that eventuality:

17 May 2004
Dear Ashraf,

When you get this letter (which was prepared in advance and is faxed to you by my wife), I am detained in Israel. I came here with the BBC to work on a TV documentary and was stopped by the Israelis, who probably want to ask me some questions about the Ashraf Marwan Affair and who was my source [who revealed Marwan's name to me]. They will get nothing from me ... but the damage to you will be substantial. I recall you telling me, when we met at the Intercontinental hotel, that what you really want is for me not to deal with this matter any more and to keep quiet (which I did). But arresting me will turn this into a major story ... Here is my advice: phone your [Mossad] friends in Israel and instruct them to release me at once.
Yours,
Ahron.
PS: A strange and ironic situation, isn't it? We become dependent on each other.

There was no need to use this letter, as in Israel I passed through passport control without a hitch; it really surprised me that the authorities there were so patient with me.

———

In subsequent weeks we spoke quite a lot on the phone. Most of the talks were short – brief exchanges – and often, even more than before, I had this nagging feeling that Marwan's reason for phoning was to keep an eye on me, to make sure I behaved myself. He would phone and ask his routine polite questions, and since I was now also the adviser on his memoirs, he always posed the occasional question about the 1973 war, which 'is information I need for the book I am working on'. His instincts were sharp and I was sure he sensed I suspected that appointing me as his consultant might have been his way to stop me from writing the book myself. I was indeed suspicious, so from time to time I would tackle him, asking questions which would help me to judge by his response or tone whether he was actually working on his memoirs. 'So what's the name of your book?' I asked on one occasion. '*1973 – What Happened?*' he replied without the slightest hesitation. 'And which period of time will you cover?' I demanded. 'From 1971 to 1973,' he shot back. 'Is it written in Arabic?' 'No, it's in English, because Arabs don't read books.' Still I was not sure and I kept on trying him.

From my diary (a summary of a telephone conversation with Marwan):

7 May 2005
Ashraf Marwan phoned … polite as ever, heavy Arabic accent. 'It's your friend,' he says. We talk

from 09.45 to 10.05 on the morning of Saturday …
Gave me his home address and asked not to send
anything to his office (home address, 24 Carlton
House Terrace, London SW1Y 5AB. Mobile:
07712777717). Asked me about what I do. I explained about the Penguin book [which I was writing on the Occupied Territories]. He congratulated
me. I've asked him about *his* book. He said, 'Half of
it is already written and it will deal with 1973 until
disengagement [in 1974].' 'When will you publish
it?' I ask, 'Perhaps in five years,' he says, adding, 'I'll
need your help.'

————

I learned to identify Marwan's swinging moods by the tone
of his voice, and at this point he was clearly upset. Perhaps it
was his worsening health condition, which he frequently al-
luded to, or his growing (unproven) suspicion that the Mossad,
his former employers, were orchestrating a smear campaign
against him.

What he genuinely found difficult to understand was how
both myself and Ronen Bergman, who was one of Israel's most
prominent journalists and quite often wrote about the Marwan
Affair, could say things in books and newspaper articles that
the Israeli censor failed to stop being published. And what upset him a great deal now was information that I'd sent him
about Bergman's new book on the Yom Kippur War, where

he implied that Marwan provided the Mossad with critical information during the course of the war itself.

In the book Bergman claims that Marwan had supplied Israel with crucial intelligence during the sixth day of the fighting. The Egyptian advance into the desert had halted. Marwan, said Bergman, now told Israel that the Egyptian advance would soon restart. Three Egyptian infantry brigades would be parachuted into the Gidi and Mitla passes, some forty kilometres east of the Suez Canal, and seventeen Kelt missiles would be launched against Israeli military targets. When this piece of information arrived in Israel, Golda Meir's cabinet was in session, discussing whether to ask Egypt for a ceasefire which, with Egyptian troops dug in in the desert after crossing the border, would be regarded as a horrible defeat for Israel. However, the information which allegedly arrived from Marwan changed everything. Now, the ministers decided not to call for a ceasefire, but instead to ambush the advancing Egyptian forces. At 6.30 in the morning of 14 October – soon after the Egyptian troops had begun to move – the Israelis hit back, destroying 250 Egyptian tanks and then – under General Ariel Sharon – they crossed to the other side of the Suez Canal. The information which arrived in Israel actually led to a great Israeli success on the ground; in many ways it saved Israel. If true, of course, then Marwan was not, as I and Zeira kept saying, a spy working for Egypt, but indeed for Israel, for if the message came from him during the war then he was helping Israel, not Egypt.

But I know that Marwan was *not* the source of this piece of information – it actually came from the other top Egyptian spy who worked for Israel, whom I have mentioned earlier in this book. This spy radioed the information using a transmitter given to him by the Israelis and his message was intercepted by a special aerial located in the Mossad's headquarters, just north of Tel Aviv. In a cruel twist of fate this spy was killed by Israeli fire during the Egyptian advance. Marwan, of course, also knew that this critical piece of information did not come from him, but he could not say so; he was just annoyed, and his suspicions that the Mossad were conspiring to destroy him grew.

Then another article in the Israeli papers upset Marwan even more: in a picture, published in *Yediot Aharonot*, a leading Israeli newspaper, Marwan is seen standing alongside Egypt's President Hosni Mubarak, under the headline: 'THIS IS HOW MUBARAK HUGS OUR SPY'. I sent Marwan the article, as I did with all pieces of information published about him. A few days later he phoned me from a cab. I immediately recognized that he was furious and hurt. Without going through his usual preliminaries, he flew into a rage, launching into a tirade of angry shouts. His voice choked as I had never heard before and he screamed at me at the top of his voice: '*Why are they [Mossad] doing it to me? Why are they taking revenge?*' When he'd calmed down, he lowered his voice and said that the photographs were old images, taken two years before and, as he regarded it, the fact that the Israelis used these images so long after they were actually taken demonstrated that the Mossad were trying to drive a wedge between him and Mubarak. When I put down the phone I was as upset as Marwan as I imagined how it must feel to be in his position.

———

6 OCTOBER 2006

It is the thirty-third anniversary of the Yom Kippur War and I am thinking of Marwan. Then the phone rings.

From my diary (a summary of a telephone conversation with Marwan):

Ashraf phoned at around 13.05 (long conversation; forty minutes or so). He used the old trick as he did before. First called and kept silent, listening to my voice to ensure that it was me on the other end. Then I disconnected and a few minutes later he phoned again (not identifying himself, of course). We talked about the weather first. He's apparently in America (so he says). Health problems 'for the last three years', but 'I am in good hands'. He asked for the name of Arieh Shalev's new book [on the Yom Kippur War] and I dictated very patiently Shalev's name (he asked me to wait while he turned off the television). He said, 'They [the Israelis] can say whatever they want ... The results [of the war] speak for themselves. [The prime minister] Golda Meir wanted to commit suicide ... The Israelis lost hundreds of tanks in the first days of the war.' Rambling, rambling, rambling and I could hardly understand how one thing was linked to the other. 'I am not superman,' he said, by which he probably meant that the deception plan in 1973 was done not only by him but by others as well. He said, 'Sadat's only mistake was to move forward [into the desert on 14 October] because [Syria's President] Assad was screaming ...' Told me about the medal he received and about Sadat's speech in which he had said that 'without this man (a reference to Ashraf) we would never have won the war'. He'll show me the English version of Sadat's speech when we meet again 'in a few months, when I am back from America'. Said that he wrote all of Sadat's speeches and they were a team of forty people whose task it was 'to feed the Conception to the Israelis [that Egypt will not embark on war before obtaining certain weapons] ... there was no single double agent ... there was Egypt', as he put it. Quite talkative: 'Keep updating me,' he said. The bottom line is that he's not going to admit that he was a spy at all; he was just part of a bigger machine that misled the Israelis.

He talks so much that I suspect that he's perhaps on medication or something and so at the end of my note I scribble: 'Marwan's in a talking mood.'

Ashraf and Mona Marwan in later years. By this time Marwan was ill and depressed, his identity as a former spy already revealed to the world

CHAPTER 6

Marwan is Dead

———

26 JUNE 2007

IT IS A THURSDAY AND I stop by at home on my way to collect my little boy from school. The telephone answering machine's light is flashing and I quickly press the button to check out the messages. There are three. I listen to the first message and when I hear Ashraf Marwan's voice my heart sinks. 'Hello, hi, I am [phoning] about your book. If you could call me back on my mobile. Thank you.' I've known Marwan for nearly five years now and this is the first time he has left a message on my answering machine. It is not his style to leave messages. He has a strong notion of telephone security. He is so careful on the phone. He is a spy – a real spy with a soul of a spy, and spies do not often leave messages on answering machines unless it is absolutely essential. I grab a chair and sit down, trying to give some order to my running thoughts. By then the answering machine is playing the next message, which was received fifty-nine minutes after the first one. 'God,' I can hear

85

myself saying out loud. 'It's him again!' It goes: 'Please, hallo can you call me about your book. Thank you.' And then the third message, received just twelve minutes later: 'Hello, hi, good afternoon. If you can call me I am the subject of your book. Thank you.' Holding my head in my hands, I sit there, my heart racing. '*Ma Kara lo*,' I hear myself saying in Hebrew. 'What's happened to him?' I run the trio of messages, all recorded within the space of seventy-one minutes, listening attentively to his tone, which I know so well, and I immediately realize that, particularly in his second message, he sounds concerned; the tone of his 'Please' reveals it all. Something is going on; but what?

The week before, I had sent Marwan an envelope containing articles about a legal battle that had ended in a libel suit filed by the former head of Military Intelligence, Eli Zeira, against the Mossad's former director, Zvi Zamir, both of whom served before and during the 1973 Yom Kippur War. In media interviews, Zamir blamed Zeira for publicly exposing Ashraf Marwan's identity, of revealing Marwan's name to me and perhaps to others too, and of thereby revealing top state secrets, breaking intelligence etiquette and endangering the spy's life. In retaliation, Zeira sued Zamir for libel – and lost. The judge found that Zeira had disclosed top secret confidential information, and the judge then produced a long report, which was published in the Israeli press and put on the internet too. In it, Ashraf Marwan's name was mentioned many times, which meant that his identity as a spy had become a matter of public – official – legal record. While I had placed Marwan in some danger by exposing him as a spy, this was still only the word of a historian; no higher power had offered confirmation of the fact. Now, with the high-profile court case between two senior Israeli officers and the judge's ruling, this was all official; for the first time, a judge named Marwan as a spy.

———

In the car back home from his school my little boy is quiet; he is a perceptive lad and he can see that I am miles away. When we get home, I put him in front of the television, close the door and climb up to my study, where I take out my old tape recorder, slip a fresh tape into the machine and check that it works properly. I had never before recorded my conversations with Marwan, knowing full well that if he realized that I was doing so he would, at once, cut off all contact with me, as he had done with Dubi Asherov, his Mossad controller. But now it is all different. Something had happened, or was about to happen, and my gut feeling was that I was reaching the climax of my relationship with Ashraf Marwan – and, anyway, I will only record myself talking to him, only my end of the line, so that I can later reconstruct our conversation.

I position the tape recorder on the desk and grab my notebook. In tense and difficult situations, and I remember it from my Lebanon war experience, I often become calmer and quieter; but now, as I dial Marwan's number, I can see that my finger is shaking and I feel my pulse in my temples. His phone rings and he picks it up at once. 'My friend,' I say, relieved to hear his voice, 'how are you?' 'I am okay,' he replies, 'and how are you? I received your envelope.' He is referring to the envelope with articles on the Zeira–Zamir legal battle; apparently, mistakenly, I had sent this envelope to 80 Park Street, W1, which was his old London address, and so it took almost a week for it to reach him. Now he is extremely concerned about his name being mentioned in the judge's report and in the press, and this is the reason he had tried to catch me and left the messages. A few minutes into our conversation Marwan suddenly asks me to call him back in two minutes, which I do but he does not answer. I persist in phoning him every two minutes and on the fourth try he picks up, apologizing that the line is faulty, and we continue our conversation.

I explain to Marwan about the judge's report but he interrupts me and cuts straight to the heart of the matter: 'What's the bottom line?' he asks. 'The bottom line is that the judge also published your name,' I reply. I ask him whether he has seen the report, but he has not. 'I have his report here,' I say to Marwan, 'but I can't give it to you. I don't want the authorities in Israel to blame me for doing things that maybe I am not supposed to do.' I myself gave evidence before the judge and he had been very clear in his warnings to me not to say anything about the proceedings: the questions I was asked, my answers – nothing at all. 'I understand,' Marwan says.

I tell Marwan that I am travelling to Switzerland on the Sunday to do some summer teaching there, and so he hastens to ask: 'Where are you tomorrow?' 'Tomorrow I will be in town ... at King's College,' I say, whereupon Marwan suggests: 'So shall we meet tomorrow?' I give him my mobile number (which he has already got) and he takes the number down very carefully and then asks me to repeat it, so that he could ring me the next day to arrange a time for our meeting and together we could go over the judge's report. When we are done I ask Marwan: 'Otherwise, you are fine? You're OK?', to which he replies: 'Just fine, apart from this headache' – by which he means the judge's report.

I feel better after the conversation. He sounds all right, in spite of his 'headache'.

———

27 JUNE 2007

My office is in the war studies department at King's College London and there I am awaiting a call from Marwan, as arranged the day before, to tell me where we could meet. Judge Or's report is in my bag and from time to time I dig it out to go over the sections I would discuss with Marwan. I am waiting and waiting with growing irritation, but he fails to phone and it is getting late. During our five-year relationship, I had grown used to Marwan's capricious behaviour. 'Agents aren't aeroplanes,' I remind myself, recalling John le Carré's words. 'They don't have schedules.' But when it passes midday, I pop up from my office to check mobile reception – reception is poor in my basement office, where I work – to see if he has called. But no; not a word from him.

At around this time, a few miles away from my office, an ambulance has been called to 24 Carlton House Terrace. When it gets there, the paramedics are directed to a little private rose garden at the back of a building, where a man is lying among the roses, still breathing, his face to the ground. He utters a few words and then he dies. It is Ashraf Marwan. He tumbled off his balcony to his death – either he was pushed off or he jumped.

Ashraf Marwan fell to his death from the fifth floor of this London building. His body landed in the little rose garden under his balcony. © Heathcliff O'Malley

Marwan's mysterious death sends shockwaves through Egypt and across the Middle East, including Israel. The region is a constant rumour mill – and speculation is rife that this was no accident, but murder. Marwan is the third Egyptian living in London to die in similar circumstances. In June 2001, the Egyptian actor Soad Hosny fell from the balcony of Stuart Tower, a block of flats in Maida Vale, after she approached a publisher offering to write her memoirs. In August 1973, El-Leithy Nassif, former head of the late Egyptian president Anwar Sadat's presidential guard, fell from a balcony in the

Ahmad *(Left)* and Gamal *(Right)* Marwan, the sons of Ashraf Marwan, pray during their father's funeral. His coffin is draped in an Egyptian flag, Cairo, 1 July 2007. © Nasser Nuri / Reuters / Corbis.

very same tower. He too was writing his memoirs. All three victims had links to the Egyptian security services. Was Marwan's death another stitch in a pattern whereby Egyptians are thrown to earth from high-rise London buildings?

———

The Metropolitan Police treat his death as suspicious, and soon well-dressed detectives march into my tiny office. The first to drop by is Detective Constable Martin Woodroffe. We shake hands and he hands me his business card, from which I gather that he belongs to Team 8 of the Specialist Crime Directorate at the Metropolitan Police. He is youngish and polite; very English in a striped suit. He asks questions and I give answers. When I try to ask him about this or that he goes all shifty, giving nothing away. But I gather that he is exploring three possibilities: that Marwan was murdered, that he jumped – although no suicide note has been found – or that he fell. Woodroffe is interested, so he tells me, in many things about Ashraf Marwan but particularly in the book he was apparently working on and for which I have been the consultant. Apparently, the only existing draft of this book had mysteriously disappeared on the day Marwan plummet-ed from the balcony of his London flat. 'Have you seen the book?' Woodroffe asks. 'Do you have it on your computer?' (He adds: 'We might need to inspect your computers, but not now.') 'No,' I say, 'I have never seen it', which, when I tell this to Woodroffe, seems to be strange; helping Marwan on it for months and years and not even seeing it once! 'I just know it exists,' I add, whereupon he shoots back: 'And how do you know that?' 'How do I know that?' I hear myself asking myself aloud, before saying to Woodroffe that in our telephone conversations Marwan would always ask questions about the Yom Kippur War to help him with his text and I had no reason to believe that he faked his questions. 'That isn't a proof that the book really existed,' Woodroffe insists, to which I have to reluctantly agree.

He also wants to know about the planned meeting which I was supposed to have with Marwan and, as he puts it, 'where *exactly* have you been around 1 p.m. on the day Marwan had fallen? Do you have witnesses to say that indeed you have been where you say you've been?' His question throws me off balance, and I feel my ears flushing and the sweat running down my back; and it gets worse as I can see that Woodroffe can sense my stress. Ridiculous, I think. *Grotesque!* Does he really suspect that *I* pushed Marwan to his death? From his bag, Woodroffe takes out a small plastic bag and he holds it open. He tells me to drop in the original tape recorded messages left by Marwan on my phone the day before he died. I also hand over to Woodroffe all the drafts of faxes I sent Marwan over the years and summaries of my conversations with him. Woodroffe stands up, we shake hands and he leaves my office. When I shut the door behind him, I feel utterly exhausted. I put my head on the desk and all I want to do is cry.

———

That the police doubted whether Marwan actually worked on his memoirs hurt, as it portrayed me in a ridiculous light. For if there was no book, then what were all my stories about being Marwan's consultant on his – by then non-existent – book that 'disappeared', according to his family, on the day he fell to his death? Thus, after Marwan's death, finding proof of the memoir's existence became an obsession for me and I embarked on yet another of my compulsive crusades to try and establish the truth behind Marwan's book! I spent hours on the phone, conducting a massive investigation to see whether Marwan had visited archives and libraries to research a book. At first it frustratingly yielded nothing, but finally I made a breakthrough. I managed to locate a certain Mary Curry, a junior librarian at the Washington National Security Archives. She, I learned, personally assisted Marwan on a visit there. I could not believe my luck and I was as thrilled as I was on that day in Tel Aviv when I finally identified Ashraf Marwan as the mysterious Mossad spy. By January, I was ready with enough information to prove that indeed Marwan had been working on his memoir, and I wrote to DC Woodroffe:

8 January 2008
Dear Martin,
As requested I attach the emails received from Mary Curry, regarding Ashraf Marwan's visit to the

National Security Archives, Washington, in January
and March 2007. You'll see that these reports strength-
en my point that Marwan was working on a book.

I attached the following letter sent to me by Mary Curry, the
Washington librarian:

We had no advance notice of [Ashraf Marwan's] arrival, he simply walked in the door on January 23rd
2007, and showed up again unannounced on March
20th and returned on March 21st. In January, he
filled out the name and address section of our Visitor
Welcome Sheet and signed it on the back. He told me
he wanted to research Egypt–Israeli relations during
the 1970s. He said he was writing a book about his life
and was looking for background information. While
I was showing him how to use the Digital National
Security Archive, he mentioned casually that he had
been the secretary to Anwar Sadat. I realized he was
an important part of history and an eyewitness to
many events. He looked at many documents. When
Dr Marwan returned in March he wanted to continue using the DNSA. He was interested in having
his own subscription. He was using a cane when he
visited us in January and March. After he left I sent
him an email thanking him for giving us two boxes
of Godiva chocolates.

Amidst all this I got a letter from a Mr Harding, a criminal lawyer representing the Marwan family:

> Dear Dr Bregman
>
> I confirm I have been instructed on behalf of the family of Dr Ashraf Marwan in relation to various matters but specifically relating to the inquest to be held by the Westminster coroner into the circumstances of Dr Marwan's death. I anticipate this will take place early in the New Year. I have been provided with your contact details by Marwan's eldest son, Gamal. He advises me that you had some contact with Dr Marwan in the weeks and days leading up to his death on 27 June. I am particularly anxious to meet if you want to discuss your contact and various related matters ...

I meet Mr Harding and his assistant at their fancy offices at Kingsley Napley in Central London. They are nice, very English, offering tea and biscuits, and explaining that the Westminster coroner, whose task it was to establish what had happened to Marwan, seemed not to be in any hurry and was taking his time. As for the Marwan family, says the lawyer, 'they are Moslem ... they wouldn't buy the suicide story'. The police enquiry, he adds, is 'sluggish and so incompetent' – so much so that he suspects that 'someone has asked someone not to investigate it properly'. The lawyer clearly thinks that the British authorities – for whom I know Marwan had spied too – are not keen for this matter to be made public. As for the missing memoir, the lawyer asks me the same questions as the police did: 'Has it existed? And who's the publisher? And why don't we have more than one copy?' The bottom line is that in due course the Marwan family's lawyers would like me to appear before the coroner and to say two things. First, that a meeting between me and Marwan had been scheduled; this, says Mr Harding, would strengthen the view that Marwan did not commit suicide but perhaps was pushed off his balcony, as people who make plans to kill themselves do not usually arrange meetings for the next day, and they do not bother, as Marwan had done, to take down telephone numbers. Second, to talk about Marwan's book that had disappeared and about which I – as Marwan's consultant on it – am perhaps the only person who can comment. Maybe, reflects Mr Harding aloud – and I can see that he does not believe it himself – there was something in the book which led to the killing; this could weaken the suicide option and strengthen the murder one, which is what the family hoped the coroner would decide had happened.

Years later, among the millions of emails leaked by WikiLeaks, I discovered the following email sent from the Metropolitan Police to Detective Edward Golian from the Major Crimes Division (Cold Case Squad), Montgomery County Police, Maryland, USA, who had tried to link the death of Marwan to another incident (the gunning down of

the Israeli military attaché Yosef Alon in Washington in 1973)
and who had asked about Marwan's book:

> Sir,
>
> Martin Woodroffe is away at present but I answer
> as the officer in charge of the Scotland Yard investiga-
> tion into the death [of Ashraf Marwan] … Our inves-
> tigation found no evidence, or material, which could
> have been considered to be Dr Marwan's memoirs.
> Many people suggested that he was writing memoirs
> but all efforts, including forensic analysis of his lap-
> top computer, indicated that this was not the case.[1]

———

17 April 2008

The police detectives come and go. This time it is DC John
Johnson, whose main expertise is murder and criminal offenc-
es; he asks his questions, takes some notes and leaves. And then
before long it is Woodroffe again, accompanied by a Keith
Bowen whose business card he hands me indicates that he is
from the Homicide and Serious Crime Command – MIT6 at
Belgravia Police Station. They have some more questions and
ask me to sign yet another statement. I ask Woodroffe whether
I should take any precautions to protect myself, given that – if
Ashraf was indeed murdered – there might be people out there
who, as I put it to him, 'might have some crazy ideas'. As usual
he is evasive, but says that he might have to visit my house to

put taps on my phone line in case someone phones whom they might want to record.

———

2010.

It is now three years since Marwan's mysterious death and at last the police investigation is over. Two separate murder squads, including Scotland Yard's elite Specialist Crime Directorate, examined the case and now it is down to William Dolman, the Westminster coroner, to decide what actually happened on the fateful day. He will conduct three days of deliberations, during which he will take evidence from the police, medics, friends, family and colleagues before making up his mind. I am dreading having to testify in front of the Marwan family and am relieved when on the first morning of the inquest Woodroffe phones to say that, after all, I will not be asked to give evidence. Apparently, the coroner is only interested in the last twenty-four hours in Marwan's life, and my role in it is in any case summarized in my signed statements to the police and the two tapes which are already with the coroner, containing Marwan's three messages he left on my answering machine the day before he died and a recording of our last conversation late on that afternoon. But before long Woodroffe is back on the line; the family's barrister, a Mr Evans, had insisted that my testimony that there was a book manuscript and that a meeting had been scheduled with Marwan the day before he died should be heard orally.

So the next morning I am at Horseferry Road Magistrates'
Court, visibly nervous, and when I catch sight of myself in
a wall mirror I can see that my face is sickly white. At the
court, I am told that my testimony is scheduled for the afternoon, so I find myself spending the entire day sitting in
a tiny courtroom just behind Mona Nasser. From time to
time I glance at her as she listens attentively as witnesses describe how her husband was seen pacing the balcony, looking down, climbing up on a pot, over the balcony railings,
'walking' into the air. Apparently, on the morning of his
death, four men were meeting on the third floor of an adjacent building, 116 Pall Mall, in a room with clear view
of Marwan's balcony. In a curious twist, these men worked
for one of Marwan's companies, Ubichem PLC; they were
waiting for their boss to join them. He was late. When they
called around midday to find out why, he assured the group
that he would be with them shortly. One of them, sitting
with the window to his left, recalled that he was startled by
one of his colleagues crying out: 'Look what Dr Marwan is
doing!' Next the coroner invites one of the medics to give
her evidence, and she then describes the body position – face
down – the few words Marwan murmured before dying, and
the cause of death, which was a ruptured aorta. Reports are
read in court and filed; one report is from his doctor stating
that Marwan had been 'under considerable stress of late' and
had lost ten kilos in two months; another report is of the
post mortem examination, indicating that antidepressants
were found in Marwan's blood. The coroner then examines

Marwan's circumstances and it emerges that Marwan had just been accepted into the Reform Club, whose members include Prince Charles and the former MI5 boss Dame Stella Rimington. Marwan had plans, it is reported in court; he and his wife Mona were due to take their five grandchildren on holiday. He had appointments. He had reasons to live. Mona sits there, so dignified, listening to all the details, not a muscle moving on her face. And what a confusing day: one minute I insist to myself that Marwan was killed, the next that he committed suicide. When it is my turn, I go up to the podium, take the oath and tell the court about Marwan's memoirs and the meeting we were due to have on the day he died and which never happened. When I walk back down from the podium to return to my seat my eyes meet Mona's and we nod to each other.

The coroner's verdict when it comes in the late afternoon is a sheer relief to the family: 'an open case', the coroner announces. That means that it has not been proven how Marwan died and that there was no evidence to support either suicide or unlawful killing. 'We simply don't know the facts, despite careful investigation,' the coroner tells the court, adding: 'There are many unanswered questions ... Did he jump or did he fall? Here the evidence does not provide a clear answer.' One of the reasons for that is because claims about Marwan's death involve, as the coroner put it, 'the murky and secretive world of espionage'.

Marwan died as he lived, mystery surrounding everything. His secret life and death remain opaque.

Followed by her son, Mona Marwan, widow of Ashraf Marwan,
leaves a London court after the first day of the inquest into her husband's
death. © Heathcliff O'Malley

An Afterthought

---

27 JUNE 2013, 1.40 P.M.

I CHOOSE THE DAY AND time with precision. Today, six years ago, while I was waiting for him to phone, Ashraf Marwan plunged to his death. I am standing at 24 Carlton House Terrace, across the terrace from the white, Grade I listed buildings that overlook St James's Park, my face pressed against the railings, through which I can see the little rose garden where Marwan died. I look up to the balcony of the fifth floor, trying to imagine how Ashraf climbed up the balcony fence, which is quite high – but then he was tall, over six feet – stepping on a plant pot, or on the air-conditioning system, and then over the rails, 'walking' into the air and falling down. I wonder: what was he thinking about when he fell? When he saw in front of his eyes the floors running faster and faster on his way down? Was he just thinking that in a split second he will hit the ground and it will all be over – his double life, the unceasing watchfulness, the loneliness? Was he thinking about his kids? About his wife, Mona? About his father-in-law, Egypt's charismatic leader President Gamal Abdel Nasser? Or did he think: well, Bregman, you can keep waiting for me at your office, but I am not going to show up for our meeting – that's your punishment, let it be on your conscience.

———

People often ask me: 'So what do *you* think happened to Ashraf Marwan?' And, quite frankly, I often ask myself the same question. When the Marwan family asked me, through their lawyers, to appear before the coroner and bolster the case that their husband and father was killed rather than committed suicide, which is a disgrace in the eyes of many in the Muslim world, I did so gladly. I think that I did deliver the goods, and I felt good about it, and even now part of me still believes that it was not suicide, but murder. Perhaps by the Egyptians, who rejected my double-agent story and concluded that Marwan betrayed them. Or perhaps it was linked to Marwan's murky business dealings – he was, after all, an arms dealer. Fuad Nasser, a former head of Military Intelligence in Egypt, when asked in an interview whether in his opinion Marwan had been killed or had committed suicide, said, 'in my view he was murdered … who did it … I don't know, but generally speaking … There's no doubt that this is an assassination operation.'[1]

And yet, I must confess that for years now there has been a little voice inside me insisting that it was not a murder but that Marwan did commit suicide after all. This nagging voice is not an abstract idea, but it has to do with a moment in my last conversation with him on the day before he died, which was strange then and is even stranger now. During our conversation I said to Marwan that I could not meet between two and three in the afternoon, as this was my office hour with my students. His response – or rather the *tone* of his words – as I thought then and more so now, implied that I should not be concerned about it as he would not show up anyway.

You – the reader – will then surely ask, so why the three messages he left and the long telephone conversation to arrange a meeting – writing down my telephone number, repeating it and so on – if he had no intention of being there? Well, it might be that this was Marwan's way of organizing his post-death story. He, of course, did not want to shame his family with a suicide – it goes strongly against Muslim tradition, and Marwan, although secular in his daily life, did care about religion. Perhaps there was also a life insurance policy, which would not be paid in the case of suicide. He knew that I would explain to the world – as I indeed did – that Ashraf Marwan meant to meet me on that day and therefore it did not make sense that his death was a suicide. Moreover, he also made sure that I could prove that we were in touch the day before he died by – uncharacteristically – leaving three telephone messages on my home phone. You might say that this is too far-fetched. Well, if you have reached this point in my story, and internalized how Ashraf Marwan functioned, then you will not – I am sure – dismiss this explanation out of hand.

Transcript of My Last Conversation with Marwan

———

TUESDAY, 26 JUNE 2007 AROUND 4 P.M.

AB: Hello … My friend?

AM: Hello, how are you?

AB: I am OK and how are you?

AM: Can you wait a minute [he's probably moving to another place].

AB: Yeh, sure, absolutely …

AM: Hi [or something like that].

AB: How's life?

AM: OK, how are you?

AB: Well, not bad working too hard as usual but … [laughing]

AM: I got your envelope.

AB: Yes, I realize that I sent it to the wrong address I …

AM: Yes … What's going on?

AB: What? The thing in Israel? Well, what happened …

[I explain about what happened.]

AM: My friend ...

AB: Yes?

AM: Can you call me in two minutes?

AB: Yes, absolutely, yes ... [speaking aloud] Two minutes later ... And ... two minutes later ... And ... two minutes later ... third time ... Fourth time ... Hi. Hello.

AM: Sorry, the line was faulty ...

AB: No, no, no, don't worry ...

AM: Are you at home?

AB: I am at home, yes ... Listen, listen, I am in town tomorrow ... if we want to meet we could meet but it's up to you ... Let me ... let me explain what happened there.

[AB continues to explain for quite a long time.]

AM: What is the bottom line?

AB: The bottom line, I say, is that ... the judge published the report ... also published your name ... You haven't seen the report?

AM: No, I haven't ...

AB: Right. OK. Yes, I can't really ... I have his report here ... erm, but I can't give it to you ... I don't want the authorities in Israel to blame me for doing things that maybe I am not supposed to do ...

AM: Yes, I understand ...

AB: Yes ... Are you in England?

AM: Yes, I am in England.

AB: Listen, I am going to Switzerland on Sunday, erm ...

AM: Where are you tomorrow?

AB: Tomorrow I will be in town at King's College …

AM: So shall we meet tomorrow?

AB: OK, let me give you my mobile.

AM: Just a minute … yes.

AB: 07941 …41 … 460 659 … now …

AM: Can you repeat it?

AB: yes 07941 460659.

AM: OK.

AB: Now, let me give you also my office number. Because my office is in the basement, my office is in the basement and my mobile doesn't work there … 020 7848 2944.

AM: OK.

AB: I'll put the report in my bag, ermm … but I can't meet between two and three …

AM: [inaudible] Where are you based?

AB: King's College … it's on Strand not far from Trafalgar Square … ermm, OK, so I'll put it in my bag … if if you want … you know … it's up to you …. if you are free we can talk about it … *but I can't leave the report*, OK? I can't leave it … Otherwise you are fine? You're OK?

AM: Just fine. Apart from this headache …

AB: Apart from the headache, yes …

AM: [inaudible]

AB: OK, my friend, all … the best … bye bye.

Acknowledgements

———

THANKS TO PROFESSOR URI BAR-JOSEPH and to Yossi Melman who, while often disagreeing with me on the Marwan Affair, have always treated me with respect, separating our professional differences and our friendship. Uri produced a superb book called *The Angel* on Ashraf Marwan and the Yom Kippur War, which I have used here. Eli Zeira, director of Military Intelligence in 1973, has always been, in spite of our thirty-year age gap, a good friend and we have shared delightful moments chatting away while tucking into the fabulous buffet at the Intercontinental hotel in Park Lane; having mentioned our friendship, I would emphasize – yet again – that Eli has never revealed to me, nor hinted or confirmed, Ashraf Marwan's identity as a spy. I have replaced the original title of this book, which was *Death of a Spy*, with *The Spy Who Fell to Earth*. The latter was the title of a piece on Marwan published in the

Guardian newspaper and written by Simon Parkin. Thanks are also due to Charlie Smith, Irene Wise, Aviva Dautsch, Stuart Proffitt, Laura Stickney, Dai Richards, Norma Percy, Daniela Richterova, Charlotte Ridings, Mark Handsley, "Madam" Caroline, Melissa Raphael, Georgia Abrams and Brian Lapping.

SELECTED BIBLIOGRAPHY

Bar-Joseph, Uri, *The Angel: Ashraf Marwan, the Mossad and the Yom Kippur War*, Tel Aviv: Kinneret, Zmora-Bitan, 2011 (in Hebrew)

Bergman, Ronen and Gil Meltzer, *The Yom Kippur War*, Tel Aviv: Yediot Aharonot, 2003 (in Hebrew)

Black, Ian and Benny Morris, *Israel's Secret Wars: The Untold History of Israeli Intelligence*, New York: Hamish Hamilton, 1991

Blum, Howard, *The Eve of Destruction: The Untold Story of the Yom Kippur War*, New York: HarperCollins, 2003

Bregman, Ahron, *A History of Israel*, London: Palgrave, 2000

—, *Israel's Wars: A History since 1947*, London: Routledge, 2010

Bregman, Ahron and Jihan el-Tahri, *The Fifty Years War: Israel and the Arabs*, London: Penguin Books/BBC Books, 1998

Gamasy, Mohamed Abdel Ghani El-, *The October War: Memoirs of Field Marshal El-Gamasy of Egypt*, Cairo: The American University of Cairo Press, 1993

Heikal, Mohamed, *The Road to Ramadan*, New York: Ballantine, 1975

Kahana, Ephraim, *Ashraf Marwan, Israel's Most Valuable Spy: How the Mossad Recruited Nasser's Own Son -in-Law*, New York: Edwin Mellen Press, 2010

Katz, Shmuel, *Soldier Spies: Israeli Military Intelligence*, Novato, Calif.: Presidio, 1992

Kipnis, Yigal, *1973: The Road to War*, Virginia: Just World Books, 2013

Nasser, Tahia Gamal Abdel, *Nasser: My Husband*, Cairo: The American University Press, 2013

Nutting, Anthony, *Nasser*, New York: E. P. Dutton, 1972

Robinson, Jeffrey, *Yamani: The Inside Story*, London: Simon & Schuster, 1988

Zeira, Eli, *The Yom Kippur War: Myth vs. Reality*, Tel Aviv: Idanim, 2004 (in Hebrew)

Articles, newspapers, TV programmes
Bergman, Ronen, 'Their Man in Cairo', *Yediot Aharonot*, 6 May 2005 (in Hebrew)

Croft, Steve, 'Was the Perfect Spy a Double Agent?', CBS, *60 Minutes*, 10 May 2009

Dayan, Ilana, 'The Last Spy', TV programme, *Uvda*, Number 9, 27 December 2007 (in Hebrew)

Melman, Yossi, 'This Doesn't Sound Like the Ashraf Marwan I Have Known', *Haaretz*, 6 July 2007

—, 'What Is Known About the Mysterious Death of Ashraf Marwan?', *Haaretz*, 28 May 2010 (in Hebrew)

Zeevi, Nadav, 'The Betrayed', *Maariv*, 28 December 2007 (in Hebrew)

References

---

1. Who was Ashraf Marwan?

1. Uri Bar-Joseph, *The Angel: Ashraf Marwan, the Mossad and the Yom Kippur War* (Tel Aviv: Kinneret, Zmora-Bitan, Dvir, 2011), 35 (in Hebrew).
2. Tahia Gamal Abdel Nasser, *Nasser: My Husband* (Cairo: The American University in Cairo Press, 2013), 97–8.
3. Simon Parkin, 'Who Killed the 20th Century's Greatest Spy', *Guardian*, 15 September 2015; Bar-Joseph, *The Angel*, 43–6; Michael Bar-Zohar and Nissim Mishal, *Mossad* (Tel Aviv: Miskal, 2010), 212 (in Hebrew); 'Ashraf Marwan: Problem Child', www.mideastwire.com/topstory.php?id=16682.

2. Marwan Volunteers for the Mossad

1. Bar-Zohar and Mishal, *Mossad*, 214.
2. On this critical moment see Parkin, 'Who Killed the 20th Century's Greatest Spy'; Bar-Joseph, *The Angel*, 56–9.

3. For a good discussion on walk-ins see Bar-Joseph, *The Angel*, 59.
4. For more about the above and why the Israelis were convinced Marwan was genuine, see Bar-Joseph, *The Angel*, 72.
5. Bar-Joseph, *The Angel*, 77; Parkin, 'Who Killed the 20th Century's Greatest Spy'; Tal Kra-Oz, 'On the 40th Anniversary of the Yom Kippur War, Israel's Top Spymasters Face Off', *Tablet*, 4 October 2013.

3. Spying

1. As quoted in Parkin, 'Who Killed the 20th Century's Greatest Spy'.
2. Moshe Dayan in a conversation with Rami Tal, 22 November 1976, published in *Yediot Aharonot*, 27 April 1997.
3. About this system, see Ilana Dayan, 'The Last Spy', *Uvda*, Number 9, 27 December 2007 (in Hebrew); also, private interview with R; Bar-Zohar and Mishal, *Mossad*, 214.
4. Interview with R; also Bar-Joseph, *The Angel*, 56.
5. Private interview with R.
6. Dayan, 'The Last Spy'; Bar-Joseph, *The Angel*, 159; private interview with R.
7. Private interview with R.
8. Bar-Joseph, *The Angel*, 49; private interview with R.
9. Bar-Joseph, *The Angel*, 157; private interview with R.
10. About this story see Ahron Bregman, *A History of Israel* (London: Palgrave, 2002), 145–8; Dayan, 'The Last Spy'; Bar-Zohar and Mishal, *Mossad*, 215–16.

[11.] Zvi Malkin played a leading role in the abduction of the Nazi war criminal Adolf Eichmann from Argentina in 1960, and in Europe kept an eye on the whereabouts of Ashraf Marwan, following him as far as Paris and beyond in an attempt to see with whom he met.

4. I Unmask Marwan

[1.] Bar-Zohar and Mishal, *Mossad*, 206; also a private interview with R.

[2.] Bar-Joseph, *The Angel*, 327–8; private interview with R.

[3.] The person who provided the king with information was a Syrian divisional commander. He was recruited by Abboud Salem, an Iraqi pilot who defected to Jordan in the early 1960s and became a Jordanian intelligence officer. Salem, who later served as the commander of the Jordanian Air Force from 1973 to 1976, was related through his wife to this Syrian spy, whom he had recruited as an agent long before the war.

[4.] Ahron Bregman, *Israel's Wars* (London: Routledge, 2010), 113.

[5.] Uri Dan, 'A Spy Artist', *Maariv*, 4 March 2005 (in Hebrew).

[6.] Ronen Bergman, 'The 'Kotel' Code', *Yediot Aharonot*, 7 September 2007.

[7.] The reasons why Sadat decided not to wait for the supply of weapons from the USSR before embarking on war against Israel were that he was tired of the continued Israeli occupation of his land and the realization that the

USSR, given her improved relationship with the US during the so called *Détente*, would not provide him with the attack weapons requested.

8. See, for example, Saad el Shazly, *The Crossing of the Suez* (San Francisco: American Mideast Research, 1980); Mohamed Abdel Ghani El-Gamasy, *The October War: Memoirs of Field Marshal El-Gamasy of Egypt* (Cairo: The American University of Cairo Press, 1993).

9. Eli Zeira, *The Yom Kippur War: Myth vs. Reality* (Tel Aviv: Idanim, 2004), 126 (in Hebrew).

10. Bregman, *History of Israel*, 142–3; also *Yediot Aharonot*, 19 September 2002.

11. Halud el Gamal, 'The Israeli Historian Keeps on Mixing Poison with Honey: Ashraf Marwan a Perfect Spy and a National Arab Hero', *Al Ahram al Arabi*, 300, 21 December 2002.

6. Marwan is Dead

1. Email sent on 3 May 2011 from Kevin Naidoo, Detective Inspector, SO15 Counter Terrorism Command, High Tech Unit at the Metropolitan Police, to Detective Edward Golian from the Major Crimes Division (Cold Case Squad) Montgomery County Police, Maryland, USA.

An Afterthought

1. Interview with Fuad Nasser, 2 June 2009, in the TV programme *Aktrak*.

Made in United States
North Haven, CT
17 October 2024

59049986R00075